Quarterly Essay

Quarterly Essay is published four times a year by Black Inc., an imprint of Schwartz Publishing Pty Ltd. Publisher: Morry Schwartz.

ISBN 9781760641399 ISSN 1832-0953

Subscriptions – 1 year print & digital (4 issues): $79.95 within Australia incl. GST. Outside Australia $119.95. 2 years print & digital (8 issues): $149.95 within Australia incl. GST. 1 year digital only: $49.95.

Payment may be made by Mastercard or Visa, or by cheque made out to Schwartz Publishing. Payment includes postage and handling.

To subscribe, fill out and post the subscription card or form inside this issue, or subscribe online:

quarterlyessay.com
subscribe@blackincbooks.com
Phone: 61 3 9486 0288

Correspondence should be addressed to:

The Editor, Quarterly Essay
Level 1, 221 Drummond Street
Carlton VIC 3053 Australia
Phone: 61 3 9486 0288 / Fax: 61 3 9011 6106
Email: quarterlyessay@blackincbooks.com

Editor: Chris Feik. Management: Caitlin Yates. Publicity: Anna Lensky. Design: Guy Mirabella. Assistant Editor: Kirstie Innes- Will. Production Coordinator: Marilyn de Castro. Typesetting: Akiko Chan.

Rebecca Huntley

It was the week before Christmas and Adelaide was alive with Labor Party people, as well as journalists, unionists, protesters, fellow travellers, interested observers and the men and women of business and civil society, there to network assertively with what was likely to be the next federal government. It was the Australian Labor Party National Conference, held every three years, at which Labor updates its platform and policies, showcases its leaders and tries to speak to both base and electorate. This 2018 conference had to radiate unity and readiness to take power. And it seemed to do just that.

It was my first conference in about fifteen years. I was intrigued to see who stalked the corridors of the Adelaide Convention Centre. Kon Karapanagiotidis from the Asylum Seeker Resource Centre was there, hoping that the party would endorse more compassionate policies on asylum seekers. Tim Winton floated in and out, attracting admiring stares from political animals who read fiction, hoping to get a commitment from Labor to protect his beloved Ningaloo Reef. These two issues – asylum seekers and the environment – have derailed Labor many times in the past twenty years, assisting in the bleeding of votes to the

Greens in inner-city Sydney, Melbourne and Brisbane, and worrying the hardheads of the Right focused on marginal seats in Queensland and western Sydney.

In 2018, Labor politicians and delegates talked about how a Shorten Labor government would make Australia a fairer, more compassionate, greener and smarter place. I thought to myself that this was, in fact, not quite true. The majority of Australians already inhabit such a place, at least in their beliefs and outlook. In that respect, they have been ahead of the political class for many years now. The role of a new federal Labor government would not be to change hearts and minds. All a Labor government would have to do – if it were to fulfil its election commitments – is update policy and law to reflect the views and desires of the democratic majority.

In the week before the conference, my father asked me about the Labor leader. What would a Prime Minister Shorten be like?

I paused to reflect, then said, "You know, it's going to be fine."

My sister retorted, "Well, there's a decline for you. The Labor Party has gone from 'It's time' to 'It's fine' in three generations."

It's not surprising that voters like my sister have scaled back their hopes for a visionary government, after the disappointments of Kevin 07. For a moment then, it seemed a modern Labor government under Kevin Rudd would fuse the traditional politics of social and economic justice for working- and middle-class people with a new politics of belief in action on climate change. And remain in government for numerous terms to cement its vision for the future.

The only grand visions Australians see nowadays are beamed to us across the Pacific, the erratic ideas of an extreme-right populism, which mostly provoke fear and loathing here. And yet the conditions exist for Labor to be something more than just an "It's fine" government, for it to do more than merely catch up with the people. There is an opportunity to renew social democracy, Australian-style. The main aim of social democracy – to "reconcile capitalism, democracy and social cohesion" – is even more relevant after the global financial crisis, the banking royal commission and with rising economic inequality.

A revived democracy is possible – if Labor is willing not only to follow through on its policy pledges, but also to enact and embed a new social-democratic tradition with environmental concerns at its core. If it has the guts to respond to public anger about corruption and corporate influence on the political class. If it has the determination and skill to use a different political rhetoric to frame the issues that matter to Australians – not just by what is merely profitable, but by what is right. And if it can muster the gumption to argue creatively and consistently that the social-democratic policies that many of us want require not only reform of the taxation system to make it more equitable, but also higher taxation across the board. That is what a truly progressive politics would look like. In many respects, it would be the expression of the wishes of the majority of Australians, who are desperate not just to "move forward," but to see genuine progress, in our country and our politics.

The views of this democratic majority – on issues such as housing, the environment, immigration and aspects of our democratic system – may or may not surprise the reader. But understood in their complexity, these views show clearly that the opportunity is there for an incoming Labor team to be bold in its approach to government, unapologetic in its advocacy for the public sector, and courageous in its leadership on the environment. Even on the vexed issue of immigration and asylum seekers, there is potential for a less defensive, more open approach. All in all, Australians are ready for reform, and more ready for the revival of social democracy than many assume.

How do we know this about the Australian people? Because the research tells us so. I am a social and market researcher, involved in the "dark arts" of focus groups, polling, surveys, and strangers who ring you in the middle of dinner to ask your view of your local candidate. No doubt my profession has been under attack for many years as contributing to the corruption and mendacity of party politics. Not only are our methods questioned, and the ways in which our work is used criticised, but the veracity of our conclusions is constantly doubted. It's common for commentators to say on election night that the polls got it wrong. Even our nearest and dearest can join in the chorus of disapproval: as a jokey response whenever a work colleague asks what his wife does for a living, my husband replies, "She's an expert in the opinions of people who don't know what they are talking about."

While it is true that some polling (namely, seat-based robo-polling) can be unreliable, there is no evidence that national political polls in Australia are inaccurate. In fact, history shows that such polls produce exceptionally accurate results, even with the transition from landlines to mobile phones and online surveys over the past decade or so. As well as many national polls, there are myriad datasets on politics, including the Australian Election Study (AES), the Australian Values Survey (AVS), the Scanlon Foundation's various reports, and issues polls such as the Essential Report, the Ipsos Issues Monitor and the Lowy Institute Poll. Increasingly, the CSIRO and like organisations are also doing substantial research on public attitudes. Taken together, this research gives a consistent and reliable picture of where the majority of Australians sit, not just on politics but on a range of issues. Thanks to compulsory voting, there is no silent majority in Australia. There is an un-silent majority, whose views are plain to discern.

But are these views being heeded by our political leaders? Often the claim is made that our politics and politicians are poll-driven. This is, on the whole, bunkum. While fluctuations in the polls might be used by political frenemies to destabilise, there is no consistent evidence that the policy agenda of the major parties has been shaped mainly by opinion polls. If such polls were influential on policy and politics, we would have made big investments in affordable and social housing, banned foreign donations to political parties and further curtailed corporate donations to political parties, invested much more in renewable energy, maintained and even increased funding to the ABC, and made child care cheaper. We would have also made marriage equality a reality through an act of parliament, without an expensive and hurtful postal survey (the most wasteful piece of market research in the history of Australia). We may already have made changes to negative gearing and moved towards adopting elements of the Uluru Statement from the Heart. We would have made euthanasia legal across the country and started the process leading to a republic. We would have put more funding into Medicare and the National Disability Insurance Scheme. We would have taken up the first iteration of the Gonski education reforms. We would be installing a world-class national broadband network. These are some of the issues on which this democratic majority comes together: topics that attract 60 per cent or higher public support if we refer to all the available surveys, a basic agreement crossing party lines, stretching from soft Liberal and Labor to Green and independent voters – and even (on some issues such as euthanasia and donation reform) to One Nation voters.

While we are on the topic of polling and trust, we should also confront the other fallacy doing the rounds: that Australians have lost faith in politics, government, even democracy itself. That trust in institutions is at an all-time low. The statement that there is a widespread decline of trust in institutions of all kinds is repeated so often that it has become a truism. It's presented without any real context or conclusions about what this might mean for our politics. Even a casual reader of our colonial history would know Australians have never really trusted politicians. So, the low trust in political parties is not surprising, and any downward trend there is unlikely to be reversed easily. Assisted by numerous royal commissions and scandals, there has also been a decline of trust in religious organisations, business groups and even charities.

According to the Essential Report in 2018, the top trusted institutions are the federal and state police (70 per cent and 67 per cent), the High Court (61 per cent), the ABC (54 per cent) and the Reserve Bank (50 per cent). Despite our cynicism, Australians still have some faith in the institutions that uphold the rule of law, direct the economy, and check and balance the powerful. Political parties are at the bottom of the trust list, according to Essential, at 15 per cent. The AVS, coming out of the Australian National University, confirms that very few Australians express confidence in the country's political parties, and that number is declining even further. In 2018, 27 per cent of Australians reported having "no confidence at all" in political parties. No more than 1 per cent of Australians expressed "a great deal" of confidence in parties on any of the four occasions the question has been asked since 1981. Furthermore, the AES shows that the proportion of Australians who agree that "people in government can be trusted" (by which they mean politicians and the public service) has declined from 51 per cent in 1969 to 26 per cent in 2016. These numbers reflect conversations I've heard in focus group after focus group over the last decade and a half. Australians see corruption everywhere and believe that almost everyone has a self-serving agenda. They are always on the lookout for the lie, the rip-off, the hustle, whether it be from a telemarketer, tradie, minister of government or minister of religion.

However, has this lack of trust in politicians and parties strangled engagement in our democratic life? I judge that it has not – yet. While Australians are disdainful of party politics, most of us are still interested in political issues. In October 2018, a few months after the Liberal Party leadership spill, an Ipsos survey found that 59 per cent of Australians described themselves as "very" or "fairly" interested in politics. The AES shows that around 43 per cent of Australians say they have some interest in politics and 34 per cent a good deal; these levels of interest have remained stable over three decades. The participants in the focus groups I conduct might not be across the detail of politics – the name of the Minister for Trade, or who said what in Question Time – but they have lots to say about the big issues that face this country. They are interested in policy but not necessarily capital P politics or the small-minded, petty squabbles they see played out in the media.

If we look at just the bare facts of voting – enrolment, participation and informality – then our faith in democracy seems fairly robust. Informality (making a deliberate or accidental error in voting which means your vote can't be counted in the ballot) has actually *decreased* in recent years. Enrolment is at 96.2 per cent of the eligible population. Since the introduction of compulsory voting in 1924, turnout at elections jumped to over 90 per cent and has remained largely stable. While there has been a slight downward trend in turnout from the 1990s, it is "so slight that it barely warrants the term 'decline'." While turnout is dependent on age, with young people less likely to vote, the AEC has found no generational effect in non-voting in Australia.

In other words, voting is something all Australians grow into, regardless of what generation they belong to. The announcement of the same-sex marriage survey in 2017 saw 90,000 new voters, most of them young, enrol in time to respond, defying those who characterise young people as apathetic, and annoying the "No" campaigners who hoped to profit from their apathy. (This doesn't mean all is well with young Australians and the current state of democracy and politics, but more on that later.) Indeed, the same-sex marriage survey is one of the best examples of Australians' active involvement in democracy. The response to a survey that was mailed to people (old-school) and not compulsory (practically un-Australian) was extraordinary: 79.5 per cent of those who received a survey submitted a response.

Some might dismiss this high level of voter engagement as a Pavlovian response to the threat of a fine and the promise of a sausage sizzle. But, as political scientists Sarah Cameron and Ian McAllister point out, "A majority of voters consistently support compulsory voting, and there has been relatively little change in these proportions since the 1950s." In fact, while support for compulsory voting has remained in the 70s for decades, a still higher percentage of Australians indicate they would vote even if it wasn't compulsory – in 2016, that figure was 80 per cent. Among all the perceived evils and ills of domestic politics Australians have pointed out to me, compulsory voting has rarely been one of them.

While compulsory voting in itself doesn't guarantee a meaningful democracy, it has the effect of creating a broad sense that voting is an important obligation (rather than a freedom to exercise or not), like obeying the road rules. It also creates a political culture that, on the whole, has to speak to the reasonable majority. Despite the focus in election campaigns on swinging voters and marginal seats, the two major political parties have to pitch to the centre. They don't have to "turn out their base," as parties need to do in the United States and the United Kingdom. Extreme policies and slogans that beat the partisan drum aren't necessarily required in a high-turnout environment. Historian John Hirst may be right when he describes compulsory voting as "the most distinctive characteristic of the Australian system." In some respects, compulsory voting is the glue that keeps the democratic majority – which is on the whole centrist and sensible – together.

And what about belief in democracy itself? How has that weathered the leadership changes of the past decade? Has the fact that the party machines kneecapped the last four elected prime ministers undermined our belief that democracy can deliver stable government? Again, much of the research seems to say no. The most recent wave of data from the AVS found that we are committed to the concept of democracy and largely believe Australia is being governed in a democratic manner.

> Almost nine in ten Australians believe that "having a democratic
> political system" is either a "very good" or "fairly good" form of
> government. Further, that percentage has been increasing since

1995. Importantly, more than half of all Australians believe it is "absolutely important" to live in a country that is governed democratically. This suggests that, for most Australians, democracy is still the "only game in town."

But are we playing that game well? Trends over time charted in the AES suggest escalating doubts. The care factor about who wins the federal election has bounced around over the years, reaching high points in 1987, 1993 and 2007 only to settle at around 65 per cent in 2016. The proportion reporting "a good deal of interest" in the election itself has steadily declined from 50 per cent in 1993 to 30 per cent in 2016. Similarly, satisfaction with democracy reached a high point in 2007 of 86 per cent – Kevin 07! – only to plummet to 60 per cent in 2016. Research commissioned by the Museum of Australian Democracy suggests that while we support the concept of democracy, we aren't happy with how it works in practice, with fewer than 41 per cent of citizens currently satisfied, down from 86 per cent in 2007.

Another worrying result – reflected in the AES – concerns the perceived effect of casting a vote. In 1997, 70 per cent agreed that "who people vote for can make a big difference." In 2016, that figure was 58 per cent. The decline could be a consequence of many things, including cynicism that big changes won't be made by either Labor or Liberal when in government, or increasing awareness that a vote in a marginal seat matters more than one in a safe seat. Or the sense that the messages voters send through the ballot box (invest in infrastructure! more funding for health and education!) aren't being heard by those elected. Indeed, the most interesting insight may be into Australians' perception of how politicians feel about them. In 2016, only 22 per cent agreed with the statement: "Parties care what people think." This figure has fluctuated only a little over the years. Despite the large increase in surveys and polls of all kinds and increasing politician/constituent communication, just over half of the respondents to the 2016 AES agreed with the statement that politicians know what ordinary people think. It seems that while voters are constantly being asked their opinion, they are not convinced they are being listened to.

So trust in political parties is low and trust in other institutions is generally declining. Voter frustration is high. And yet there hasn't been an equivalent loss of faith in democracy – in theory, if not in practice. It is extraordinary that despite peak cynicism when it comes to politicians, we still support the processes that see them elected to run our governments.

Accompanying this faith in democracy is a belief in the vital role of government. I would argue that the public believes in this role more strongly now than at any time since the 1980s. Understanding that enduring belief is critical to understanding social democracy, Australian-style, and how it might be revitalised.

Australians find it hard to define what it is to be Australian. They are probably better at identifying what is un-Australian. For some, the WorkChoices
policy John Howard took to the 2007 election was un-Australian. Refugees
who "jump the queue" are un-Australian. Giving jobs to migrant workers or sending jobs overseas is un-Australian. Big apartment blocks are
un-Australian. Getting rid of penalty rates is un-Australian. And banning
Christmas carols at primary schools is un-Australian. We generally still place
the ideal of fairness or a fair go at the heart of what this nation is about.
People struggle even more when it comes to describing the best kind of
government for our country, the kind that will guarantee that fair go for
the greatest number of people. Reflecting on everything I've ever heard
from every Australian in the research I've conducted, I might distil it to
this: a good government is one that makes it hard for people to buy a gun
and easy for people to get health care. That seemingly bald statement says
a lot about Australian attitudes to the role of government and the purpose
of democracy. And about why the notion of social democracy remains
attractive to the majority of citizens.

Defining "social democracy" today is no simple task. The social democratic tradition can refer to both non-communist and labour parties of the
left in European and English-speaking countries like Australia, but also to
a political system that gave birth to the welfare state and a Keynesian,
interventionist approach to economic management. Broadly speaking,
a social-democratic politics seeks to ameliorate, rather than dismantle,
capitalism in the interests of equality and social justice. It conceives a critical role for government: to protect people, especially the working and
middle classes, from the vagaries of the free market and technological dis-
ruption. As the political scientist John Keane points out, social democrats
across the world aimed to reduce inequality caused by market failure by
pursuing the right to vote; a minimum wage; compulsory industrial arbi-
tration; unemployment insurance; publicly funded education, health care

and transport; public service broadcasting; and public pensions. At the heart of social-democratic thinking from the very beginning was the idea that many things in life – the things that make life worth living – can't be reduced to a dollar value on capitalism's spreadsheet. Keane writes that:

> Social democrats acknowledged the ingenuity and productive dynamism of markets. But they were sure that love and friendship, family life, public debate, conversation and the vote could not be bought with money, or somehow be manufactured by commodity production, exchange and consumption alone.

In other words, social democrats knew that, as the feminist Eva Cox puts it, we live in a society, not an economy.

But that was then, this is now. Keane takes up the global story of how many social democrats made their peace with capitalism and embraced the Third Way:

> A decade ago, most people interested in politics associated the words "social democracy" with business-friendly governments, lower taxes, economic growth, high wages and low unemployment . . . It represented a progressive vision of market reforms, new public management and rising consumption, a shift from savings capitalism to a capitalism of easy lending, the triumph of a new era of "privatised Keynesianism" . . . The reputation of social democracy has since been damaged. The phrase nowadays connotes things much less positive: career politicians, scripted speeches, intellectual emptiness, declining party membership, discredited defenders of "too big to fail" banks and austerity.

Perhaps with Britain particularly in mind, Keane concludes that the much-lauded "Third Way has turned out to be a dead end."

In Australia, too, the original promise of social democracy has not been fully realised and the vision of a fair society has been compromised. First, there were the economic reforms of the Hawke/Keating government, including deregulation and privatisation. Even left-wing economists acknowledge that some of these reforms were necessary. I have neither the space here nor the expertise to judge whether each and every one was good or bad for the Australian people. I merely point out that an undeniable outcome of these reforms was that public confidence in the state as efficient, effective and profitable – as the best way to deliver essential services to the whole population – was weakened.

The other recent problem for social democracy in Australia is that it hasn't delivered on its promise to significantly reduce economic inequality. While Australia hasn't seen the squeezing of the middle class and the rise in poverty that America has, we should nevertheless be disappointed at current levels of economic inequality (should we ever feel triumphant when we are better than America?). A recent report from the Australian Council of Social Services showed that income inequality in Australia is now above the OECD average, with the top 10 per cent of wealth holders owning 45 per cent of all wealth and someone in the top 20 per cent owning seventy times more wealth than someone in the bottom 20 per cent. This inequality has been driven by several things, including low wage growth; unaffordable housing; the gender pay gap; inadequate investment in health, education and infrastructure; inequities in the tax system; and insufficient welfare payments. These conditions have not solely been created by the policies of the conservatives. Labor has brought them about at different times as well.

Finally, social democracy has been damaged by the already mentioned lack of trust in the political class. John Keane observes that the initial successes of social democrats in parliaments led to the rise of the mass political-party machine, which "soon fell under the spell of cliques and caucuses, backroom men, fixers and spinners." When social democrats become political animals, their values can go out the window. Toxic factionalism can develop, such that maintaining factional power becomes the main and sometimes sole criterion by which decisions – even crucial ones of policy – are made. Keane argues the machine men (and, yes, they are mostly men) in social-democratic parties have "not only ... lost public support. They have become objects of widespread public suspicion or outright contempt." At the same time that factions have become more entrenched and powerful, so too has party membership declined. Keane notes that:

> In spite of the decision (in mid-2013) to allow rank-and-file members to cast a vote for the party's federal leader, [ALP] membership ... is still at or below what it was in the early 1990s. Civil society organisations such as the RSL, Collingwood AFL Club and Scouts Australia all have far bigger membership than the Labor Party.

There are further problems. From the outset, social democracy struggled to fully take up the fight against racism. Indeed, some versions of social democracy around the world have involved – even relied on – extreme nationalism, xenophobia and explicit exclusion of non-whites. The environment, particularly climate change, poses another, newer challenge to traditional social-democratic values. Social democracy emerged when better rights for working people dominated many of its claims on the state. Its rhetoric and imagery privileged men employed in forestry, mining, construction and manufacturing – all industries reliant on pillaging the natural world. The values and icons of environmentalism stand in stark contrast to this. Indeed, since the 1980s we've seen clashes between "laborism" and "environmentalism" play out in the caucus and cabinet rooms of Labor governments, and in inner-city seats, where voters swing mostly between the ALP and the Greens.

Given all the problems, past and present, with social democracy, why bother to make the effort to revive it? Because few of the social and economic problems that social democrats sought to combat have disappeared; they have only mutated. Social-democratic forms of government – specifically the Keynesian welfare state – arose in part as a response to insecurity and world collapse in the 1930s and 1940s, as a reasonable middle path and alternative to fascism and communism. Today, insecurity is rife, the threat of global collapse just as acute, but the threats are not bound by sovereign borders: they include the loss of job security in a globalised world, the fear of international terrorism, and the effects of climate change. And before you think these ideas are too abstract, too highfalutin, to be registered by "everyday citizens," think again. In the aftermath of the GFC, and after a particularly nasty spate of bushfires and floods, I talked to a group of sixty-something men in suburban Brisbane. One of them said, "That's our future now, extreme economic events and extreme weather events." Add lone-wolf terror attacks on Australian soil and you have a disturbing trifecta.

In 2010, a few years after the fall of Lehman Brothers precipitated the global financial crisis, the historian Tony Judt addressed a large audience at New York University on "what is living and what is dead" in the social-democratic tradition. He acknowledged the difficulty of such a task after decades of privatisation, the devaluing of the state, the loss of connection of people to "the commons" through policies pursued by centre-right and centre-left governments around the world. But nevertheless, such a revival was possible. He said that social democracy emerged out of the experience of war, the threat of totalitarianism from the far right and the far left's assault on liberalism. In fact, social democracy was a way for liberalism to defend itself. Its aims were clear: greater equality, the creation of a strong public service and public institutions, and the notion of a collective purpose. He said that probably the most radical ideal of social democracy was not any one policy idea or program but the idea that we should ask of any decision government might make: is it right? In other words, we should apply an ethical rather than an economic framework to the actions of government. Social democracy has been tarnished in recent years precisely because it has too often reinforced the economic over the ethical. It asks: is this decision productive, efficient, profitable? rather than: does it substantially improve the lives of the greatest number of people now and in the long term? To revive social democracy in a place like Australia, we have to go back to basics – or so argued Professor Judt. What are the social goods we believe in? And what is the good society?

As luck would have it, anyone seeking to rework social democracy in Australia for current times has an important ally: the Australian people. John Keane has made the point that the success of social democracy in its initial decades was so impressive and the absorption of its demands into the mainstream of politics so rapid that it "gradually had the effect of turning every fair-minded person into a social democrat." This is certainly the case for the majority of Australians. If we explore their attitudes to the purpose of democracy, the role of government and, more recently, the economy, this becomes very clear.

Australians support democracy. But to what end? Research conducted by the Centre for Policy Development (CPD) in 2018 found that around one in three Australians believe the main purpose of democracy is to "ensure that all people are treated fairly and equally, including the most vulnerable in the community." For average wage earners, this rises to nearly one in two (48 per cent). Only 19 per cent of those surveyed thought the main purpose of democracy was to "ensure people are free to decide how they live their lives." The CPD concluded that these results reveal much about Australians' attitudes to government.

> First, it's about more than voting governments in or out. The bargain is *purposeful*. It's about ends (policy aims and outcomes) as well as means (elections). Second, the bargain is *big*. Unlike Americans, Australians want an active government that boosts equality and protects the most vulnerable. Australians believe government can be a "productive partner." Australians have consistently believed essential services like health, schools, social service payments to the elderly, and economic infrastructure are under-resourced. They value these services because of their community benefit, not because of any personal dividend.

The CPD's findings are backed up by the research for the Museum of Australian Democracy. When asked to select the aspects of democracy they liked most, respondents' top choice was "Australia has been able to provide good education, health, welfare and other public services to its citizens." In other words, Australians take a largely pragmatic or practical, rather than ideological, approach to democracy. The point of democratic government is to do things for people, not to prevent government from doing things to people.

I believe there can be enormous strengths in such an approach. As I argued in my book *Still Lucky*, fairness matters more to Australians than freedom. John Hirst was not the first critic of our national character to observe that Australian democracy is largely undoctrinaire. "There are no grand Australian statements about democracy," Hirst wrote in 2002, "but the values that underpin it flourish in society at large."

And those values – of fairness both for individuals and the collective – are necessarily flexible and relaxed in their application rather than static commandments capable of being enshrined in a revered document.

If the purpose of democracy in Australia is above all to secure equality, then we expect government to pass laws and pursue policies that fulfil this purpose. It is government's role to provide services (health, education, welfare) that provide all of us with the best possible chance to contribute to both the society and the economy. Government also has the right, to a certain extent, to ban, restrict and heavily tax things that are not only bad for citizens but also cause broader public harm (consider guns and cigarettes: Australia has been a world leader in controlling these products). That's because our expectations of democracy presuppose a government that intervenes in both the private and public spheres (or perhaps it is the other way around: our expectations of government shape our attitudes to the purpose of democracy). "Is there a political response that will help all of us?" is our characteristic question.

Years ago, I watched as Australians enthusiastically adopted household water restrictions as a response to drought and low dam levels; indeed, I watched as they complained about those restrictions being lifted. I found a similar response when it came to plastic bags. For years, participants in my focus groups commented that they were harmful to the environment and wanted government to step in to restrict their use; with the greater and greater anxiety about plastic waste over the past eighteen months (driven in part by TV shows like *The War on Waste*), those desires have increased. This confirms for me that if you can convince Australians that something is harmful to the collective good, governments will have a stronger licence to act than they might assume.

Way back in 1930, the historian W.K. Hancock described Australians' attitude to government in ways that are still highly relevant. He wrote, "Australian democracy has come to look upon the State as a vast public utility, whose duty it is to provide the greatest happiness for the greatest number. The results of this attitude have been defined as *le socialism sans doctrines.*"

Hancock argued that new countries (let's read that now as new imperial colonies of immigrants) demand strong government in order to master an obstinate environment. A dispersed and struggling population looked to government to help, "because there was nowhere else to look." He wondered whether once "occupation has slackened into settlement" and Australians begin to feel "cramped for elbow room," they would still look first to the government to solve their problems. Well, yes, they have and they continue to. Anxieties about overcrowding in cities and immigration levels, fear of a big Australia, have not dented our reflexive turn to the state to intervene when issues arise and need to be solved. Indeed, they have increased this tendency.

Research over the last two years reveals clearly what Australians want government to solve. These are the issues, naturally enough, that they feel have been left to drift for too long or where there has been political gridlock: addressing the challenges of an ageing population, investing in infrastructure, transitioning to renewable energy, ensuring access to affordable housing and making sure the economy benefits everyone. No matter whom I interview, health, jobs (including lack of job security and wage growth) and the economy almost always rank in the top five concerns. People wonder whether governments are far-sighted and committed enough to invest in the infrastructure sorely needed to maintain current population growth. And while the strength of the economy is often discussed, participants worry more and more about whether the economy as currently organised can deliver a fair share for all.

Concerns about economic fairness create an opportunity for those seeking to revive social democracy. Hirst writes that "the desire for equality in social, political and economic realms has been a major force in Australian history." That's true, but looking closer we can discern peaks and troughs in popular opinion when it comes to questions of fairness in the economic realm. I have witnessed important changes in attitudes, stretching from just before the global financial crisis to the recent banking royal commission. These changes go beyond the mere decline of trust in banks and the financial sector. Before the GFC, Australians were more focused on bashing the supermarkets than the banks. (While there was concern about the banks' tendency to be overgenerous with lending, especially with credit cards, when it came to bad corporate behaviour people were more worried about the supermarkets' high food prices and treatment of beleaguered farmers.) The crisis proved to us that, as Keane writes, "Free markets periodically cripple themselves, sometimes to the point of total breakdown," and "unregulated markets generate bubbles whose inevitable bursting bring whole economies suddenly to their knees." And yet Australians pointed to the regulatory framework governing the four big banks here as the shield (along with the mining boom) that protected our country from a recession. In the years that followed, as corporate profits stabilised and even rose, but the electorate felt the pinch on wages and the rising cost of living, I witnessed increasingly cynical, even downright contemptuous, responses to arguments about the merits of big tax cuts for business, the justification for large CEO salaries and bonuses, and the supposed benefits that flow to citizens and consumers when public assets and services are privatised.

Then the banking royal commission proved that the regulatory shield that protected the Australian economy from the GFC couldn't protect Australian consumers from being ripped off left, right and centre by the big banks. Now the majority of Australians believe more needs to be done by government to regulate the financial sector, including harsher penalties for wrongdoers (such as prison terms) and more funding for the watchdogs. Yet the avalanche of bad behaviour revealed by the royal commission has done something more than this. In the past year, it's become a reference point in discussions about bad corporate behaviour generally and the justification for more government oversight and better laws. *"Even if there are laws, big business gets around them. Look at the banking sector." "Look at the profits of those banks, even with the scandal of the royal commission. Imagine what we could do if we invested those dollars in infrastructure?"*

It's even led people to ask whether corporations ought to be excluded from some sectors of the economy altogether. When it comes to superannuation, for example, the public just doesn't buy the idea that retirement savings are better managed by private rather than public or not-for-profit organisations. A 2017 survey conducted for Industry Super Funds found that 70 per cent of people want super to be not-for-profit. In focus groups, Australians feel decidedly uncomfortable with banks being allowed to invest further in super. Consider the following sentiments from middle-income earners: *"If banks increased their power over super, the next generation would suffer. It would be bad for Australia to see that happen. What are we working hard for? The banks?" "They make enough money as it is, why do they have to make money off this? It's supposed to feather our nests for the future, not theirs."* In today's backlash against unconstrained markets, in our questioning of the profit motive as the path to the common good, we see a resurgent belief in the state as a necessary guarantor and regulator, as the architect of our collective security.

Related to this is a new call for government to skill up and step in when it comes to many social services. This can clearly be seen in the CPD research, which found that:

> Three quarters of Australians think it's important for government
> to maintain the capability and skills to deliver social services directly
> rather than pay private companies and charities to deliver them.

Fewer than one in ten think this is not important. What's more, Australians rate services delivered by government as more accessible, more affordable, of higher quality and easily more accountable than those delivered by private companies and even by charities.

Who should pay for these services? We should. At least that's what we see in the Australian Election Study. In 1969, when asked whether they preferred less tax or more spending on social services, 65 per cent of Australians favoured less tax. In 2016, the figure was 35 per cent. Over the same period, the proportion of Australians asking for more public money to be spent on social services increased from 15 per cent to 32 per cent. In a recent Essential Report, 61 per cent of respondents were prepared to pay some level of increased tax for more spending on services. The CPD found strong levels of public support for a raft of revenue-raising moves, including closing corporate tax loopholes (81 per cent), raising the high-income tax rate (70 per cent), putting a carbon tax on polluting businesses (59 per cent), and an indirect tax on alcohol, sugar, tobacco and gambling (products Australians recognise cause enormous societal damage and costs to the public health system). What's notable about this is that Australians must know that corporate interests would respond to these tax increases by saying they have no choice but to charge higher prices for everyday items. Support for these measures could indicate we are mostly unperturbed by this threat. We are so angry with corporations that we are prepared to call their bluff. Taken together, all this research shows that the majority of Australians have not swallowed the line that free markets and lightly regulated corporate interests produce wealth for all.

This research also raises the critical question: do voters always want two mutually exclusive outcomes, namely more public spending and lower taxes? No doubt attitudes to taxes are where the rubber hits the road when it comes to the renewal of social democracy. Australians want more government involvement and investment in a slew of areas, but are they prepared to pay higher taxes *themselves* to support this? The policies

Australians support – world-class broadband, better health and education, the National Disability Insurance Scheme and so on – demand enormous amounts of state revenue.

The AES suggests that in theory most Australians now give priority to investment in public services over tax cuts, but it's also clear that they don't want that burden to be carried by lower- and middle-income earners. The 2018 Essential Report showed overwhelming support (79 per cent) for the government's middle- and lower-income tax cuts. Only 37 per cent agreed that workers earning $40,000 and $200,000 should pay the same rate of tax. The most popular tax reforms were making multinational corporations pay their fair share (84 per cent support) and stopping people with family trusts splitting their income to avoid tax (58 per cent). There was quite strong opposition (65 per cent) to increasing the tax rate for workers earning under $87,000 a year. Many believe there are fundamental inequalities in the tax system. Given this, it's hard to see how the majority will agree to income tax hikes to fund the social-democratic policies they support unless these inequalities are comprehensively addressed.

If I were to choose one policy area where attitudes to the role of government and the market have changed most dramatically, it would be housing. Over fifteen years of focus groups, I can't think of a topic that has provoked more comment across generations, genders, states, city versus country, or class lines. The decline of the great Australian dream of home ownership has taught us not only that the market can't be trusted to deliver fairness and equality, but also that government needs to do more and not less to fulfil democracy's promise.

In the middle of 2017, I found myself occupying an easy chair in an apartment on Sydney's leafy and affluent North Shore, talking to three generations of women about their attitudes to housing. The three women — for the purposes of anonymity I'll call them Margaret, Louise and Cate — were welcoming and talkative. The apartment belonged to the grandmother, Margaret, aged in her early eighties and still in good health. It had an elevator and was within walking distance of the shops. The strata fees were reasonable. Margaret considered herself to be extremely lucky when it came to her housing arrangements at this stage of life. She had married a clergyman and they had lived for many years in church-provided accommodation. She and her husband had bought the North Shore apartment outright with their savings years ago, with the intention of spending their retirement there. Her daughter, Louise, lived a few suburbs away with her partner. A teacher at a private high school, she had been divorced, and now owned a townhouse with her new partner and an investment property in the inner west. Finally, there was Cate. Single, highly intelligent and articulate, Cate was a nurse who lived in a studio apartment (in other words, a large room with a toilet and shower hanging off it) close to the inner-city hospital where she worked in emergency, often on night shift. I didn't ask them their views about party politics — I wasn't there for that — but their attitudes to housing policy were pretty clear and not in any way conservative. They all believed something big needed to change.

First of all, they believed in greater investment in social and affordable housing. Margaret had grown up around Blacktown and had seen how important the public housing there had been for families trying to get ahead. "A lot of people are just in unfortunate circumstances. Without public housing those people would have really suffered, their health would have suffered. Public housing isn't just great, it's an absolute necessity." Of course, support for social and affordable housing in theory is one thing; wanting both in your own neighbourhood is another. And yet all three believed social and affordable housing should be dispersed throughout cities and towns rather than concentrated in areas of social disadvantage. Louise said, "*The local council has every right to have a mixture of people in the area. It's healthier for people in the schools to have a mixture too.*"

Margaret was particularly worried about the younger generation. All her grandchildren were well educated and hard-working and yet she saw that housing security was out of their reach. She was dismayed that when she died, she could only pass on a fraction of what was needed for all of them to buy a home. All three women felt the current housing market made our society even more unequal, especially across the generations. They thought all levels of government had a part to play in addressing these inequalities. These women supported a policy to make affordable housing mandatory in all new developments. "*The developers make the money. They aren't hard up for a buck. They should be forced to do that.*" They also believed there should be further restrictions on foreign investment in residential property. "*Investors buying all these units. They come along with all this money, downsizers and foreign investors. They may not even live in it. The government can do something about that.*" And interestingly, they also believed there should be changes to negative gearing (the practice of investing borrowed money in an investment property so that any loss can be claimed as a tax deduction). "*We shouldn't be negative gearing. Even though we did it.*" The women veered between anger to resignation over the course of the discussion. Margaret reflected: "*We had it so good. My daughter did, as well. I guess we expect the Great Aussie Dream. That's not there for my granddaughter. We just have to adjust.*" But then later she railed against the unfairness of a system that helps people who already own houses to accrue more. "*People are falling through the cracks in a place where wealthy people are getting a lot of breaks.*"

One of the people who was arguably falling through the cracks was Cate. She wanted to be close to the hospital so she could get home as quickly as possible after night shifts. She hinted at bad experiences with shared accommodation and the tiring nature of the commute when she had lived an hour's train ride away from work. When she found her current digs, there was fierce competition for it, with other renters offering up to $30 a week more than the advertised price. The landlord saw that Cate was a nurse at the hospital and benevolently gave her the lease at a slightly reduced price. But even that lucky break didn't make renting sustainable for Cate. On a junior nurse's salary, the rent was still considerable, making saving very difficult. She told me she had two options: move overseas to a place where rent is cheaper, or get a boyfriend. "I don't see myself buying in Sydney. I might just leave the country. And being single is a big problem. I always think all my problems with housing will be solved if I had a partner. My friends with partners are so much better off."

Margaret, Louise and Cate were just one intergenerational trio I interviewed for a larger housing research project. I met men and women in different cities and states, living in regional and suburban areas. The responses were remarkably uniform. Despite some continuing stigma, there is strong support for more investment in public housing. There is concern that renters are being exploited by landlords. To provide essential services, we need affordable housing for essential workers. We need to rethink both stamp duty and negative gearing. We need pathways to housing security that aren't just about owning or short-term renting. And we can't let the market be controlled by developers, real estate agents and landlords. We need all levels of government to play a bigger, more effective role in making the housing market more equitable.

As I've noted, housing has been a prominent topic of conversation in focus groups since I started my research career. In my book on Generation Y (Australians born in the 1990s), many of the sixty or so young adults I interviewed nominated housing affordability as the top political issue facing their generation, along with terrorism and climate change. That book was published well over a decade ago. These young adults were on the whole more educated than their parents and grandparents and just as hard-working. And yet even modest aspirations – owning an apartment before turning thirty-five – felt out of reach. It was not like that for my generation, Gen X.

After 2000, I listened to countless Australians discuss the merits of the first home owner's grant, a one-off cash subsidy for eligible buyers. While some credit was given to governments for recognising the uphill battle faced by first-home buyers, this was mostly eclipsed by doubts about whether it was an effective measure. Was it simply increasing the already high cost of property? Was it exacerbating the housing bubble? Concerned Australians questioned whether lumps of cash of this kind were the best possible intervention in the market. Mostly they felt that changes needed to be more structural in nature, benefiting those most in need and not lining the already bulging pockets of property developers.

Over time, I have also seen attitudes to homelessness shift (to some extent). In the past five years, participants have started to comment on a growing number of people sleeping rough on the streets of our capital cities and even some regional towns. While they often ascribe the increase to broader problems with drug abuse, mental health and family violence, they also wonder whether the unaffordability and scarcity of rental accommodation is making things worse. Occasionally people remark that they know people or know people who know people who are almost permanently couch-surfing or sleeping in their cars. A 2016 survey by Launch Housing found views differed on the causes of homelessness, but respondents clearly placed the responsibility for the issue with all levels of government. Answering a question where they could choose a number of options, 64 per cent believed state governments were responsible, 57 per cent the federal government and 37 per cent local government. Compare this to the 39 per cent who chose "homeless people themselves." Interestingly, "all members of the local community" was almost as popular a choice, at 36 per cent. When people were asked if the government was doing enough to address homelessness, only 14 per cent agreed, and 57 per cent disagreed. In other words, most of us believe an issue like homelessness requires a state and community response, rather than merely self-help.

Concerns about housing affordability continued to build in the years after I finished my Gen Y portrait, until just after the global financial crisis, when I began to notice a shift. People started to consider a more radical measure – namely, a rethink of the taxation of property, especially negative gearing. It was intriguing to me that some of the people who floated this idea had investment properties or aspired to own one. In the lead-up to the 2016 federal election, when Labor had announced a new policy to abolish negative gearing for new investors wanting to buy existing properties, I was conducting focus groups in Sydney's inner city with swinging voters under forty. I spoke to a mix of well-paid young professionals looking both to buy and to invest, a few homeowners, and young people struggling to find and afford rental properties close to work and friends. Housing affordability was by far the most important issue across all groups. One person reflected the mood of his peers when he said: "*If you saw food or health care went up at the rate that housing has, it would be considered a national disaster and they'd step in and do something.*" Some had landed on a compromise: they rented in the area they loved and owned an apartment in a suburb much further from the city. And yet this compromise was not ideal. They didn't particularly want to be landlords, while also feeling insecure in their own residential arrangements.

When it came to solutions, a few felt governments couldn't do much. "*I don't really know what a government can do, because it's private enterprise, isn't it?*" "*If the government was like, we've got this plan for housing affordability, I don't know if I would believe it.*" For these sceptics, the first home owner grant scheme was still front of mind. Many questioned whether increasing the supply of houses would solve the issue. Maybe houses would be built at greenfield sites on the city's periphery, hours away from where they worked and played. Or apartments would go on the market, only to be bought up by investors at high prices. "*They've got a big development planned on the other side of the road, five or six hundred thousand for a studio. I wouldn't call that affordable. But essentially, there's more supply. You'd think it would drive down prices, but no, it won't.*" "*With no limits on investing, there's no way to see if these are going to people who want to live in the area. It could just be investors who are going to charge rent.*"

Other participants were clear about what government could do: local government could encourage the building of more reserved accommodation for students and low-income earners, and state governments could invest more in public housing and improve rental laws to curb the bad practices of landlords and agents. They also thought that further restriction of foreign investment in residential property was a good idea, along with imposing limits on credit for property investment loans and the phasing out of negative gearing. This group had noticed Labor's proposed changes and was generally in favour. "*I thought Bill Shorten's announcement on the whole negative gearing [thing] was quite good. I guess everyone's been talking about how they're making property more available to younger generations … but there hasn't been any real policy behind it other than let's just keep building.*"

It was the Hawke government that introduced negative gearing in 1985. The aim was to encourage investing, increase the supply of rental properties and stimulate the economy through construction. And to relieve the pressure on public housing. It's a policy that has enjoyed bipartisan political support for a long time and also – so policy-makers assumed – support from the public. For a long time, any politician criticising negative gearing was leaving themselves open to the rebuke that they were robbing mum and dad investors and punishing aspiration and ambition. That has now changed: it's clear that the ultimate value of the current policy is being seriously questioned by voters. In 2018, the Essential Report asked: what effect will restricting negative gearing have on house prices? Twenty-four per cent thought it would lower them, 21 per cent thought it would increase them, 27 per cent thought it would make no difference and 29 per cent said they didn't know. That's hardly a ringing endorsement of the current arrangements. Rather, it represents an electorate divided about the benefits of the policy and what might happen if it were to change.

What of those mum and dad investors? Was providing housing for the next generation the dominant reason for purchasing an investment property, or was there something else? That was the central question in a research project I did in early 2018, which involved a survey of the general public and interviews with parents with negatively geared properties and their kids. It turned out that while many of the parent investors hoped there would be something left in the inheritance to pass on to the next generation, the fear of running out of money before you run out of years was the driving force behind property investment. Property is the real retirement plan, with super on the side; the kids had mostly to fend for themselves in the immediate future. And the kids themselves didn't hold out much hope for inheriting even in the long term.

On negative gearing, there was undoubtedly a divide between investors and non-investors. However, most investors said that while negative gearing helped to make their investments more affordable, they felt they could afford to keep their properties even if they could not access the tax break. In many cases the refunds they received helped pay for luxuries, not essentials. "*We could probably have got just a loan through a bank and bought the property outright and positively geared it. If negative gearing wasn't available, we probably still would've done it.*" "*All I know is we get a free holiday from the taxes.*" Those who supported changing the policy felt that this would make it easier for their children to buy a home in the future, while those who opposed tended to argue that it would have adverse consequences for the entire housing market and broader economy (rather than simply their personal financial situation). Notwithstanding the role that negative gearing plays, most investors said that they could service their investments without it, especially if they could be convinced it would make housing more accessible for the entire society. "*I would be quite happy to see it removed. To make the market more accessible to a variety ... like your working-class man.*" Overall, 55 per cent of non-investors said that they would support changing negative gearing even if it meant house prices would fall slightly. The figure for investors was 35 per cent. All the research taken together shows that this once unassailable policy is now under a cloud. If you are "stuck" renting or have no aspiration to invest in a property, then support for getting rid of negative gearing is reasonably high. Opinion is divided about the effects of such a move, with the majority of Australians not convinced it would have a negative (or any significant) effect on the market.

The great Australian dream of home ownership formed under conditions of higher wages, relatively low-cost housing and lack of interest from foreign investors. The renovated Australian dream of home security could be delivered under new arrangements informed by social-democratic values. That means no more one-off grants that inflate the profits of property developers, or piecemeal offers to increase supply or release more land. It means changing the laws around renting, ensuring developers deliver affordable housing as the cost of doing business, developing different affordable and social housing solutions, and getting rid of some of the tax breaks that benefit people already in the market. It means involvement by all levels of government and more regulation, not less. Owning your own home has long been seen as a rite of passage in this country, the reward for hard work and a place in which you build a family and create a community. In the face of rising homelessness and generational inequality, Australians are demanding that Menzies' great Australian dream of home ownership undergo a dramatic renovation.

Access to public housing was part of the original claim on the state made by social democrats inside and outside parliaments. But what of the other challenges to social democracy I mentioned previously, namely attitudes to race and ethnicity, to the environment and the climate crisis?

Over time, climate change has become the defining issue for voters judging a prime minister's leadership skills and character. In 2007, Prime Minister Howard's failure to acknowledge the threat posed by climate change (coupled with his pursuit of WorkChoices) precipitated the loss of both a general election and his own seat. "I think [John Howard] stuffed up with two things – IR and greenhouse. With greenhouse, suddenly everyone got interested and he hasn't kept up. With IR, he has bitten off more than he could chew. With greenhouse he hasn't changed, but the public has changed. With IR, he wanted change, but the public didn't." Kevin Rudd's notorious retreat from the emissions trading scheme undermined his credibility, not just on environmental issues, but as a leader with any convictions and the ability to rally his closest colleagues to his cause. "I voted for Kevin Rudd. And then he went and did that backflip. I don't believe in climate change, but I believe he believed in it. Now I don't know what he believes in." Julia Gillard's shift from "no carbon tax under my government" to introducing a carbon tax in order to secure minority government not only earned her the moniker "Juliar" but reinforced the perception she was just a power-hungry deal-maker. "She had to bend over backwards to get in with the Greens. And they got the carbon tax. How is she going to get anything done with the Greens to the left and the independents to the right? She'll do nothing just to stay in power." Tony Abbott's "stop the carbon tax" and climate change denialism reinforced the perception of him as negative and belligerent. "Abbott's modelling himself on the US Republicans, attacks all the time but never really says anything."

When Malcolm Turnbull was Opposition leader, his attempts to steer the Coalition towards full acceptance of climate change saw him booted out, which earned him some admiration from the electorate. "I admired Turnbull for that. He stuck to his guns and they got rid of him." "All the Libs hate Turnbull because he's a bit left, like he believes in climate change. They won't want him in charge." Expectations that his elevation to PM would stop the to-and-fro over climate change in the parliament ended in swift disappointment. "I had great hopes for Malcolm Turnbull and what that might do to the party, but he's been a massive disappointment. *He seems to just be toeing the party line with the environment." "He is a leader of the party, not a leader of the nation."* Turnbull's ousting was seen as both an indictment of him as a leader, and of his party. *"Malcolm was shot down for being too ambitious. Now we have a leader who is fighting for coal."* And even though climate policy hasn't been problematic for Labor in Opposition, voters have registered Shorten's two-facedness on Adani. *"Shorten can change his mind on a mine based on an election in another state. He says one thing to the inner city in Melbourne and another thing to people in Queensland."* As a political leader today, if you can come up with an environmental and energy policy, get your own people to agree and then get out of the party room intact to argue the merits of your position to the public, well, that's an achievement in itself. Climate change is the policy that can pose the biggest challenge for leaders, as it requires a deft hand in managing the schisms within your own party and convincing the public of the need for short-term sacrifice for long-term gain.

Over the past decade or so, as our federal parliament has struggled time and again with energy and climate policy, we have seen countless polls, surveys and research reports on public attitudes to these topics. Most of them have shown that only a very small segment of the community, sometimes less than 10 per cent, think the climate isn't changing. For the rest of us, who believe that it is, the critical question is: what is causing the change? The 2018 Essential Report showed that 63 per cent of us think climate change is happening *and* is being caused by human activity, 23 per cent think it is a natural process and 13 per cent don't know. On whether the government is doing enough to address climate change, Essential found 53 per cent think our leaders are not doing enough and 24 per cent think they are. The 2018 Lowy Institute Poll showed 59 per cent of Australians (up five points since 2017) believe "global warming is a serious and pressing problem" about which "we should begin taking steps now even if this involves significant costs." Almost all Australians (84 per cent, up three points from the previous year's survey) say "the government should focus on renewables, even if this means we may need to invest more in infrastructure to make the system more reliable." Only 14 per cent say "the government should focus on traditional energy sources such as coal and gas, even if this means the environment may suffer to some extent."

One of the most useful pieces of research on attitudes to climate change was commissioned by the CSIRO (still one of the most trusted government organisations in the eyes of Australians). Nearly 17,500 Australians were surveyed regularly from 2010 to 2014. The CSIRO found just under 80 per cent thought climate change was happening. On average, 62 per cent of those people believed human activity accounted for these changes to the climate. This figure did not shift over the survey period, despite the constant political ructions. Interestingly, the respondents were inaccurate when it came to predicting the views of their fellow Australians:

> The prevalence of the view that climate change is not happening was overestimated by people of all opinion-types. On average, respondents predicted that 23 per cent of Australians were of the opinion that climate change was not happening, when fewer than 8 per cent of our respondents were of this opinion.

So while political and media battles on climate change may not change public opinion dramatically, it seems they do shape our opinions of what other people think. We have, perhaps, mistaken the fights in parliament as a reflection of community division. Finally, the CSIRO report found that people think big-polluting countries, multinational corporations, wealthy countries and the government are most responsible for causing climate change. Perhaps this is why there is such broad support for investment in renewable energy, protection from invasive species, increased investment in public transport, and restrictions on development in vulnerable areas – all forms of government action.

This is the broad community view, but what about conservative voters? Given the Coalition's history on climate change and the environment, it's worth drilling down further. On the question of whether climate change is natural or human-caused, the Essential Report found that 57 per cent of

Liberal and National Party voters opted for human causation. On the question of whether Australia is doing enough to address climate change, 32 per cent believed our leaders were doing enough. There are a number of ways you could read these figures. Yes, conservative voters are less likely than Labor voters to believe climate change is caused by human behaviour and less likely to think government should do more to address the issue. However, these numbers don't reflect the kind of climate change denial and love of coal expressed by a significant and powerful bloc of politicians in the LNP. You've got close to 60 per cent of Coalition voters saying climate change is caused by human activity and only just under a third saying the government is doing enough.

Over the years, I've noticed some consistent sentiments among conservative voters. While they might question the science of climate change and oppose a measure such as a carbon tax, that doesn't necessarily mean they are sceptical about a renewable energy future. They may well be the ones who have solar panels on their roofs and support government rebates to encourage further uptake of the technology. They may have big concerns about the future of the Great Barrier Reef and the health of our river systems. They may be opposed to coal-seam gas, especially in places of natural beauty or areas important to food production. Even these climate-change deniers in the LNP base aren't caressing lumps of coal in their lounge rooms.

(I note, in passing, that it is difficult to know exactly how many federal Coalition parliamentarians are climate-change deniers. Research by Tim Beshara from the Wilderness Society shows a clear record – in Hansard and other public comments – of climate-science denialism from fifteen Coalition members. This can be anything from saying carbon dioxide is not a pollutant, or humans are not affecting the climate, to using the phrase "so-called climate change." There are many more than this fifteen who oppose any climate policy action without explicitly doubting climate science. There are others who are more like climate-attribution deniers – who, for instance, might deny climate change is affecting the

Great Barrier Reef. Perhaps we need to take the 2017 comments from John Roskam, the executive director of the Melbourne-based Institute of Public Affairs, at face value. In an interview, he said that most Liberal politicians share his doubts about climate science. "More than 50 per cent are solid sceptics and more than 50 per cent feel they need to be seen to do something.")

And finally, what about the all-important undecided or swinging voter? It is not true that only rusted-on left-of-centre voters care about the natural world. The Labor Party ginger group LEAN crunched the numbers from the latest AES data and found that 47 per cent of the electorate saw environment or global warming as "extremely important," ahead of taxation and superannuation, equal with government debt. Around one-fifth of the electorate, or 2.5 million voters, said the environment or climate change was the first or second most important issue in deciding their vote. Of those voters prioritising environmental issues, Labor was the party of choice, with 6.3 per cent voting ALP, 5.4 per cent voting Green and 5 per cent voting Coalition. The research I've done in the last two years, in particular with undecided and swinging voters, shows environmental issues like opposition to coal-seam gas and concern about deforestation, worries about water and air quality, food security and the transition to an energy market that relies primarily on renewables, come up in general political discussion and are important issues in deciding their vote. In other words, environmental issues (including climate change) are important to voters across partisan divides as well as to voters who describe themselves as swinging or undecided. Which means a political party ignores these issues at its own electoral peril.

So, we shouldn't confuse the gridlock on climate and energy policy (and extreme debates on these issues in some parts of the media) as reflective of the public discussion. This is not a matter of right versus left. Lack of action on the environment – and recognition of climate change as a genuine future threat – is a mainstream concern, one of the issues that binds together the democratic majority. Increasingly, voters expect government action, specifically by the federal government. They expect leaders to lead, and they judge them more broadly as leaders by their decisions – or indecision – in this area.

What of the social-democratic tradition? Green politics is everywhere and not going anywhere any time soon. It poses, as John Keane writes, "a fundamental challenge to both the style and substance of social democracy," because it requires left-of-centre leaders to reconcile protection of the natural world with protection of jobs, not to pit these two goals against each other, as has often been the case in Labor history. Keane goes on:

> How viable is the hope that red and green can be mixed? … Might the old and new be combined into a powerful force for democratic equality against the power of money and markets run by the rich and powerful?

I would argue that it can. In early 2018, I conducted a study on environmental protection across three states. The groups deliberately excluded anyone who voted Green, as well as anyone who said environmental issues were most important in determining their vote. The groups were made up of centrist, even conservative voters who liked spending at least some of their spare time outdoors in nature. The findings were pretty consistent. The environmental issues of concern were mostly clean air, water and soil, as well as the path we might take to a renewable energy future. There was shock about the state of the Great Barrier Reef and that the koala might still be a threatened species. There was concern about the deterioration of the green spaces they grew up with, local camping grounds or just the impact of bad city planning and urbanisation on their neighbourhoods and cities. People on the whole blamed big corporations for this environmental mess, but also the politicians who received donations from these corporations. They wanted more government action and thought that consumers and citizens played an important role through their own behaviour, including whom they decided to vote for.

These groups were more than prepared to sanction new laws to deal with environmental issues. I asked participants to rank the environmental problems we face in order of importance from 1 to 9. The list included everything from extinction of animals to deforestation to climate change. Surprisingly – at least for anyone who assumes that Australians worry about too many laws and red tape – "weak or ineffective environmental laws" was often ranked first or second and was almost always in everyone's top four issues. *"I put weak environmental laws. Looking at what's happening with the Murray-Darling, it's a joke. It's not working for any of the players involved." "The onus is on the government to say this is what you can and can't do. Everything else falls under weak laws." "The laws drive what you can and can't do. They create responsibility."* While people admitted they had no idea what environmental laws there were in Australia (other than those barring littering and dumping), they assumed that whatever was in place was inadequate or not being enforced. *"We hear about new national parks but then we hear about a new coalmine. We aren't even protecting our greatest asset. Then all the starfish in Port Phillip Bay. All the forests going, all the wildlife disappearing. Do we have tough enough laws or are we just letting the corporates do what they want?" "If you have money, you can get around those laws. Like the Adani mine."* The sentiments expressed in those groups were not an anomaly. Throughout the year, in suburban Melbourne and Brisbane (including in the all-important marginal seats), undecided and centrist voters told me similar things.

So, the majority of Australians believe the climate is changing and the majority of that majority believe humans are causing this. Environmental issues are not just a concern of left-of-centre voters; centrist and even conservative voters worry about these issues and believe governments need to do more. They are so concerned about this that they are prepared to support new laws and more restrictions on corporations in order to meet the environmental challenges that face us. Environmental issues can be absorbed into a renewed social-democratic vision for this country. Not just because the people demand it, or the precepts of modern political leadership require it, but because neat distinctions between protection of the environment and protection of the living standards of working- and middle-class people no longer hold. The public recognises that if we don't tackle environmental problems and climate change more broadly, in the end food, water and energy will be more expensive. As one man in one of my focus groups just after the 2007 election put it, "If nothing's done about the environment, Australia will become a Third World country."

However, the hard and urgent task of placing environmental concerns at the centre of social democracy requires more than just new laws and better enforcement, more solar panels and fewer plastic bags. It requires the kind of mobilisation of people and communities, assets and resources, governments and infrastructure usually reserved for a world war. It includes, undoubtedly, more state revenue-raising initiatives, including a price on carbon. If social democracy is about collective security, climate is close to the ultimate threat. But that realisation has taken too long to sink in. For many years, when I discussed the threat of climate change with groups, even those who believed it was real and endorsed government action sometimes bristled at the language of crisis and impending doom. Advocates for change were chastised for alarmism. "Climate change is going to be bad for us but not that bad anytime soon." "Think of all the times they've predicted disaster of one kind or another, and nothing has actually happened." For years, while belief in climate change remained steady, it was difficult to impress on Australians the need to act quickly on the climate crisis without being accused of employing scare tactics.

Just recently, something has shifted. Last year, when I asked groups about the main benefits of a healthy environment and taking action on climate change, the overwhelming first response was around health: mental, physical and social health relied on a healthy environment. But the second one was "staying alive in the future." Participants spoke in terms of survival! Many in the groups also recognised that when it came to transitioning to a low-carbon economy and halting the rate of species extinction, time was running out and there was a high cost to inaction. There was a new tone of urgency: "Climate change ... it has the *potential to impact our way of life." "Losing the animals, the circle of life." "When it's gone, it's gone."*

Australians are slowly getting it. Our way of life is changing. It isn't just that you can't let the kids run through the sprinklers in the backyard anymore, or that there are fewer bugs on the windscreen after a night-time drive. The Australian summer – traditionally a time of best-selling novels and drinks, family and friends – is being transformed into a time of tension and worry. There is anxiety about unprecedented weather events threatening houses and food chains, record temperatures taxing the health of older Australians, family pets and young children and sky-high electricity bills putting pressure on household budgets. In early February of this year, the novelist Richard Flanagan wrote about the fires that tore through the Tasmanian bush as the end of a way of life Australians had previously taken as a birthright. Australians were, he said,

> living in a frightening new world where summer is no longer a time
> of joy, but a period of smog-drenched dread that goes on week after
> week, and it seems inevitable, month after month. Whole commu-
> nities have been evacuated and are living in evacuation centres or
> bunking down with friends and families. Those that remain live in
> a fug of sleeplessness and fear, never knowing when the next ember
> attack will occur or a nearby fire will break containment lines, a
> gut-clutching terror of wind, smoke and heat. Volunteer firefighters
> find themselves no longer fighting fires for a week but for a season.
> Government is confronted with the extraordinary cost of fighting
> fires of this size and scale for months. This would seem to be the
> new normal.

As a community, we are inching towards recognition of the scale of the threat climate change poses to our safety and security. If there is the same lag between community attitudes and government action that we've seen on so many other issues, then all is lost. What we need is extraordinary and consistent displays of leadership: not just to accurately describe the threat but to paint a picture for citizens of what addressing it might involve. A mixture of sacrifice, selflessness, courage and adaptation. This is a message that many will resist unless they are assured that the most fortunate – particularly those in corporate Australia – are prepared to do as much as the rest of us, if not more.

Of course there is a darker side to public concern for the natural world. It's a rare discussion group on environmental issues where the topic of immigration doesn't come up. Participants don't just worry about the numbers of people in Australia causing environmental damage, they worry about the kinds of people. The values they bring from overseas where people are used to bathing in dirty water, living in litter-strewn streets and breathing polluted air. People who are capable of eating one of those fairy penguins that scramble onto the beach every night on Phillip Island (one young woman in a Melbourne focus group once expressed this fear about the intentions of some Chinese tourists she encountered at the famous Penguin Parade). There is a green vision of Australia that includes protecting this country from foreign investment, foreign money, from foreigners altogether. On this view, asylum seekers are like infected fruit or a Hollywood celebrity's pet dogs. The threat they might cross our borders unmonitored sparks fears of disease and environmental catastrophe. While environmental concerns need to be at the heart of the social-democratic vision, they can also trigger fears that echo the racist rhetoric of the social democrats of old, who argued for a working man's paradise as long as that man was white.

As noted, from the outset social democracy struggled to fully take up the fight against racism, to consider questions of colour and ethnicity. There are many critics who argue that it still fails this test. They point out that social democracy in Nordic countries has succeeded with small, relatively homogeneous populations. When these countries undergo the stress test of an increase (dramatic or not) in asylum seekers or migrants generally, the broad agreement on values starts to buckle. Some even argue that the social-democratic values and policies of the Nordic countries – which we in Australia often point to when we think about progressive reform – actively rely on racism and exclusion.

Describing how Australians feel today about immigration and asylum seekers is a trickier exercise than explaining their attitudes to the environment. The topic of "immigration" is so emotive that raising it can pinball people into discussion of a wide range of topics – everything from changing the date of Australia Day to investment in infrastructure. When you ask a question about immigration in a survey, you can find yourself measuring all manner of things, including people's sense of belonging, their views about democracy and government, and the gap between rich and poor.

The Scanlon Foundation's research on immigration is always the best local starting point from which to understand these complex attitudes. The Scanlon data shows that we continue to see ourselves as an immigrant nation, that immigration and multiculturalism benefit the country and will continue to do so in the future. In 2018, 82 per cent of those surveyed agreed with the proposition that "immigrants improve Australian society by bringing new ideas and cultures" and 80 per cent agreed that "immigrants are generally good for Australia's economy." Consistent with other surveys, the 2018 report found concern about the level of immigration rising in the last two years. However, support for a cut in immigration remains a minority viewpoint. And when the significance of this issue for respondents is factored in, as many surveys fail to do, the rise seems less concerning. In 2018, only 8 per cent of people surveyed put immigration and population in their top five concerns.

One of the reasons why untangling Australian attitudes to immigration is so difficult is that reputable polls and surveys seem to show different things. While the data from Scanlon supports a positive story about immigration in Australia, other surveys reveal greater anxieties. The 2018 Lowy Institute Poll shows a nation divided on migration levels, with a slim majority (54 per cent) saying "the total number of migrants coming to Australia each year is too high," 30 per cent saying it is "about right," and 14 per cent saying it is "too low." The Australian Values Study also reflects this community division, with 45 per cent agreeing that the government should continue to allow immigrants to come to Australia so long as there are jobs available, while 46 per cent believe the government should place "strict limits" on who moves to Australia (with only 2 per cent saying we should prohibit all migration here). An Ipsos poll showed similar results last October. And a recent poll by the Australian National University found that only three out of ten Australians believe the nation needs more people.

What this says to me is that while the majority acknowledge increased immigration has brought many benefits in the past, they are worried about the current rate and future consequence of more people coming to Australia. That equates to a concern not just about the kinds of people who might come here (terrorists and penguin-eaters), but also about whether governments are ready and able to invest in the infrastructure needed to service new arrivals. The anxiety is a reflection of lack of trust in our political leaders as much as it is a reflection of anxiety about cultural change. Indeed, in the ANU poll almost nine out of ten surveyed agreed that the high cost of housing was a reason to limit Australia's population growth. (That's why taking a social democratic approach to housing may help address social democracy's blind spot on immigration and race issues.) All in all, it is extraordinary that despite everything – the rapid growth in the size and ethnic make-up of our cities and the relentless media and political commentary on immigration levels and boat arrivals – the support for immigration (with caveats) still holds up.

Much of the anxiety around immigration in the past twenty years has focused on asylum seekers, particularly boat arrivals. The Scanlon Foundation research actually found concern about asylum seekers has declined over the past four years, as the boats stopped coming, but the issue itself clearly divides the community. Recent Essential Report data shows, broadly, that around 20 per cent of the community think the approach of the federal government to asylum seekers is too soft, 20 per cent too hard, and 40 per cent just right, with the rest undecided. When it comes to closing offshore detention centres like Manus and Nauru, again there is division, with Essential showing Australians to be almost equally divided between keeping all asylum seekers on Nauru indefinitely, bringing only children and families to Australia, and closing the entire place and bringing all asylum seekers onshore for processing.

In all my years of listening to people talk about immigration (and it has been almost as popular a topic as housing), one recent moment encapsulated the very Australian attitude to asylum seekers. It was mid-2018 and I was in suburban Brisbane, talking with undecided conservative voters, many of whom were past or potential Liberal National Party voters. I raised the topic of asylum seekers, and the response was fascinating. There was strong support for boat turnbacks (to deter more boats arriving and stop deaths at sea) and mandatory detention (to ensure border control). There wasn't necessarily strong support for an increase in our intake of asylum seekers, but nor were there calls for a decrease. People were focused on the process, rather than the numbers. Some expressed confusion about why there is such an emphasis in politics and the media on boat arrivals. *"It's such a small percentage of people coming by boat. A real terrorist would get on a plane. What are we going to do, stop the planes?"* There was, however, strong opposition to offshore detention in Manus and Nauru. *"I don't agree with this indefinite detention. The mental health of people is an issue. Not knowing how long is very detrimental. They are treated like prisoners when they aren't." "It's not humane and it's a waste of money. It's a broken system. It doesn't take that long to sort out who is a refugee and who isn't, but they've been there for years now."* People were opposed to offshore detention not just on humanitarian grounds (right or wrong), or on issues of cost-effectiveness and the burden on the taxpayer (the usual neoliberal frame for right or wrong), but because it was uncertain, unpredictable and *messy*. If you got in the queue, even if you jumped the queue, you should know when the queue ends and your number is up. These Australians objected to offshore detention largely on the grounds of perceived procedural unfairness. What a fine example of the depths of the Australian love of an orderly queue, of the emphasis we put on control and oversight!

Around the world we have seen countries with social-democratic values challenged by issues of migration and asylum. People in these mostly prosperous countries have been withholding consent to any further

intake of migrants out of a mixture of racially inspired fear and resentment and well-founded concerns about whether their country's social
safety net and infrastructure can withstand the pressure of a larger population. Similar tensions are evident here at home.

The Scanlon research shows that our commitment to a multicultural
society remains relatively stable despite attacks from all sides. But other
data shows anxiety and division about the overall pace of immigration and
the arrival of asylum seekers by boat. Developing a compelling argument
for a less racist, more diverse and more welcoming Australia is difficult in
a country with our practical approach to democracy and human rights. At
present, we have little more than the idea that more consumers are better
for the economy. Similarly, arguments against offshore detention are hard
to develop in a country so focused on procedure, rules and fairness – arguments, that is, which go beyond a concern about the slow processes of
bureaucracy. Judt's claim was that the radical edge of social-democratic
thought is to ask of any government decision "Is it right?" That's a hard
question to pose in a country like Australia on an issue like asylum seekers.
This is precisely because offshore detention and boat turnbacks seem a fair
response to the actions of "queue-jumpers" and people-smugglers. It is
because cutting back immigration seems the best way to protect our social
safety net, our unique natural environment, our local jobs and our peace-
ful, suburban neighbourhoods – what we treasure about the Australian
lifestyle. Stop the boats, save Medicare and protect the koalas.

I wish I had easy answers for how a renewed social democratic vision
might incorporate a more open, progressive approach to asylum seekers
and racism. I do know that our democracy needs more advocates – men
and women with lived experience of racism – to help answer the questions, what are the social goods we believe in? What is the good society?
When social democracy was born in Australia, left-of-centre parties,
unions and progressive governments were run by white men. If social
democracy is to be reborn, the midwives need to come from diverse back-
grounds. And yet our parliaments remain stubbornly white. Since 1988,

the proportion of Australians born overseas has risen from 22 per cent to 33 per cent, but their representation in parliament remains at 11 per cent. George Megalogenis argues that if we are to find new solutions to persistent problems, especially concerning race and immigration, we need to change the face of the political class:

> Australia will struggle to reconcile this complexity while the major political parties continue to appeal to their tribes, with the Coalition relying on white male voters, and Labor on cosmopolitan females. Targeting these groups does not win over the nation at elections; ultimately, it leaves the parliament gridlocked and undermines faith in democracy … To break the cycle, Labor and the Coalition need to build new electoral bases that unite young and old Australia. They can only do this by opening their doors to candidates that better reflect who we are: more Asian, more diverse in gender and experience.

Instituting the Uluru proposal for an Indigenous Voice to Parliament would be another direct way for government decision-making to be tested and scrutinised by men and women with experience of racism. By addressing the righteous demands of the people who have been let down most by Australian democracy, it would also boost the Australian people's faith in government as a force for civic progress.

The final obstacle in the way of reviving social democracy is the problem of politics itself. How can a social-democratic party pursue genuinely progressive reform if it refuses to reform itself and confront the plethora of current problems to do with funding, influence and equal representation? It can't. We need to renew the democracy in social democracy.

Townsville had changed a lot since I'd last visited. In the space of five years, the picturesque north Queensland town had taken a beating, with the closure of Clive Palmer's nickel refinery and the slowing down of the mining boom (in previous visits over a decade I'd encountered numerous fly-in, fly-out workers whose families were based in the town). During the day, as I walked around, local residents at the café, hotel and bookstore told me how things were going in the area. Not well. Youth unemployment was a serious problem, the town seemed depressed, no one was spending, and social problems like vandalism and ice addiction were fuelling fears of a crime wave. Later that night, as I conducted focus groups, the vital importance of reforming politics in this country really hit home.

As we talked, I handed out a sheet of paper to each person with a list of measures to improve the pay and conditions of workers. I asked them to say if each reform was, in their opinion, a good or bad idea. And then whether it was likely the reform would happen. Overall, the response to the ideas was very positive; many of them were based on a notion of more government interference in the market and greater oversight and punishment of corporate wrongdoing. So preference was high. But probability was low: many of the participants thought the reforms were pretty unlikely to be made, even by Labor governments. Why? Because of the influence of corporate money on the two major parties and the revolving door between the political class and the corporate class. One man – formerly a supervisor of a ward at the local hospital, now working security at the same hospital after it was privatised – put it this way: "It's a vicious circle. The politicians look to the corporations to get jobs when they get out of politics. And their staff, they want the jobs in the corporations too. They aren't going to piss those guys off with policies like that if they want to be hired down the track." It wouldn't have surprised this man when, a few months after we met, research was released showing one in four Australian ministers go on to work for lobbyists or special interest groups.

If social democracy has been damaged by the lack of trust in the political class, then any renewal of social democracy will require not just new policy, but different ways of doing politics. That means reform of democracy, election funding and political parties. My Townsville encounter was not a one-off. In almost every piece of research I've conducted in the last two years, I've seen mounting evidence of an electorate that understands the connection between the policies that get pursued by governments and the business of party politics. "*The pollies hang on to coal and oil because that is where their funding is coming from.*" "*Politicians and business are one and the same.*" "*Those political donations are coming from the polluters to the politicians.*"

These qualitative findings are mirrored by the quantitative work of the Australian Election Study, which shows a big increase in Australians agreeing with the statement "big businesses have too much power" – from 60 per cent in 1967 to 74 per cent in 2016. Only 9 per cent of us believe there is very little corruption in politics and only 12 per cent that there is little in large corporations. The CPD found in 2018 that 65 per cent of Australians think lobbyists have too much influence over our politicians. And Ipsos found that three in five Australians believe their country's economy is rigged to advantage the rich and powerful. (Perhaps this is why there is no consensus about which party is capable of managing a fair tax system, one that makes corporates and the super wealthy pay their fair share; when this question was put to respondents to the Essential Report last year, 32 per cent favoured Labor, 32 per cent favoured Liberal and a significant 22 per cent believed there would be no difference.)

It would be a mistake to dismiss this as the paranoia of people without power. And it is not only a question of outright corruption. As the academics Carmela Chivers, Danielle Wood and Kate Griffiths point out:

> Money in politics is regulated to reduce the risk of interest groups "buying" influence. Explicit *quid pro quo* is probably rare: as the saying goes, "You never bribe someone when you need them." But the

risk is in more subtle influence: that donors get more access to policymakers, or their views are given more weight.

We seem to have had a uniquely bad mix of laws in this country when it comes to donations to political parties. This is particularly the case at the federal level (all states except Tasmania have made good reforms over recent years). As Chivers, Wood and Griffiths explain:

> Under Commonwealth regulations, it can take up to 19 months for donations to be made public ... Only donations of more than $13,800 are required to be disclosed. And there is no requirement to aggregate donations, which means an individual donor can make a series of donations below $13,800 without disclosure. The result is a huge amount of money in the federal system that we know nothing about. Parties received more than $100 million from undisclosed sources in the two financial years spanning the 2016 federal election ... Donations can also be filtered through associated entities of the parties. This makes money (and influence) even more difficult to track.

To give just one example, the gambling, alcohol and tobacco industries donated $14.1 million to the major political parties over a decade, with the amounts given spiking during debates about the alcopop tax and gambling reforms. Concerns about this state of affairs are even harder to dismiss when politicians themselves are telling us there is a problem. In June 2018, as part of a Senate inquiry into electoral funding and disclosure reform, the Australian Greens recommended a sweeping ban on donations from developers, banks, mining companies and the tobacco, liquor, gambling, defence and pharmaceutical industries. Recent media reports indicate the ALP is looking at laws that would impose a $4000 cap on donations, which would lock out both large corporate and union contributions. During his period as Special Minister of State, Senator John Faulkner released a paper on election funding. It recommended disclosure of donations above $1000, prohibiting foreign and anonymous donations, limiting the potential for donation splitting across branches or different units of parties, real-time disclosure and tougher penalties for breach of electoral law. In a speech to the Light on the Hill Society in 2014, Faulkner argued that, "Spiralling costs of electioneering have created a campaigning 'arms race,' heightening the danger that fundraising pressures on political parties and candidates will open the door to donations that might attempt to buy access and influence." He argued that without these reforms public concern that political parties are more accessible and more responsive to large donors than to their own constituents would increase exponentially. "Elections must be the contest of ideas, not the battle of bank balances," Faulkner stated.

Naysayers who argue that such issues don't interest the punters under-estimate the intelligence of the Australian people. A September 2018 Essential Report showed 82 per cent want an independent federal corrup-tion body that will monitor the behaviour of our politicians and public servants, with no significant difference in support for this measure among Labor, LNP and Greens voters. People who argue we can change policy while leaving the political power structures in place are either naive or self-interested.

Protecting our electoral and democratic processes from corruption and undue influence seems a long-overdue task. Reviving social democracy requires us to go further. Indeed, young voters are demanding something more. While the strong involvement in the same-sex marriage survey among young Australians was a good sign, all is not well with the rising generation. Since 2012, the Lowy Institute Poll has included a question on attitudes to democracy, which has revealed a markedly different perspective among younger voters than older. In 2018, the poll showed only 47 per cent of voters aged eighteen to forty-four years say democracy is preferable to other forms of government, compared with 76 per cent of those aged forty-five and above. The Museum of Australian Demo-cracy's research shows that Generation X is the least satisfied with the way democracy works (31 per cent) compared to Baby Boomers (50 per cent). While the Australian Electoral Commission might say that voting is something Australians grow into, regardless of generation, there may well be a generation gap in how voters feel about the outcome of their vote. This is not the same as saying young people don't care about politics. A group of academics argue that the perception young voters are apathetic is both erroneous and unfair. Instead, they point to a global trend:

> Since the 1990s popular concern has accompanied considerable evidence of the withdrawal of young people from electoral politics in liberal-democratic states. That evidence includes falling voting rates, declining membership in political parties and civic organizations in major jurisdictions including the UK, USA and Australia ... Many young people no longer engage in electoral politics because they have little or no faith in the capacity of contemporary politicians to listen to them or to engage with issues they consider important ... The withdrawal of many young people from conventional (i.e. electoral) politics has been identified by political scientists as a looming problem often described as a "legitimacy crisis," a "crisis in democracy" or democratic disconnect.

Reversing that democratic disconnect requires more than new anti-corruption laws. It requires new ways to involve citizens in all levels of government. The Centre for Policy Development found that 71 per cent of Australians believe ordinary citizens should have a greater say in setting the priorities of government. And the same research found that 68 per cent of Australians would support involving citizens on parliamentary committees. I've had some experience watching deliberative democracy models at work, including citizen juries. Deliberative forums seek to break through the partisan and professional domination of policy and problem-solving by recruiting a broad and interested segment of the public and involving them in the process. They mostly involve small groups of people who come together, hear from and question experts, and arrive at a collective resolution on the way forward. In Australia they have tackled issues as diverse as bicycle lanes, third-party insurance, road safety, obesity, cat and dog management, climate change, the republic and a proposal for a high-level nuclear waste facility in the South Australian desert. I believe they have something to offer governments and communities looking to move away from an "announce and defend" approach to a more collaborative style of politics.

A renewed form of social democracy is there for the making. The majority of Australians would not only support it, they are demanding it, as seen in their attitudes to housing, the environment and democratic reform. Such a renewal would build on history and capitalize on recent shifts in public opinion – the backlash against neoliberalism. Of course Labor is the best-placed party to do this: apparently unified, chastened by the trauma of the Rudd/Gillard years and lucky to face a Coalition so dysfunctional that it decided to cancel parliament for months on end rather than risk assembling in one room. Pundits from all sides assume a Labor victory at the next election is a foregone conclusion. The size of the victory is all that's in question. And so people are asking, what will a Shorten Labor government do? I am asking instead, what *could* a Shorten Labor government do?

Bill Shorten's speech at the National Conference in Adelaide was, by all accounts, a success. Some protestors interrupted before he started, highlighting their opposition to the Adani coalmine and offshore detention. Shorten handled it well. "I know these people are well-intentioned, but the only people they are helping is the current government of Australia," Shorten told the crowd. He promised $6.6 billion to subsidise rents for low- and middle-income earners, including for key workers like nurses, police, carers and teachers. He announced that a new Labor government would strengthen penalties for employers and make it easier for staff to reclaim withheld superannuation payments. And he committed to a new environment protection agency and 50 per cent more renewable energy supply by 2030. He told the party faithful that Labor's biggest challenge was not to beat the Liberals or win back votes from the Greens, but rather to restore faith in democracy and the role of government. "Our deeper opponents are distrust, disengagement, scepticism and cynicism," he said. At the conference, Labor committed to finding a home for those detained on Manus and Nauru, but did not promise to end offshore detention. Shorten spoke of the need for more Indigenous parliamentarians and party members. While factional conflict was kept to a bare minimum, the Left failed in its push to raise the level of the Newstart unemployment allowance. Even John Howard agrees on the need for an increase, but Labor merely promised an "urgent review" within eighteen months of winning government. The only vote at the entire conference was for a Bill of Human Rights, moved by the Left, which failed to pass.

In the focus groups I've conducted since he became party leader, participants have struggled to find words to describe Bill Shorten – or at least, positive ones. His main problem, judging by what I hear, is that he is a mystery box – hard to figure out and therefore trusted even less than the average politician. He doesn't do well in preferred prime minister polls (even against the uninspiring Scott Morrison). In surveys, respondents describe him as "untrustworthy," "disappointing," "lacks charisma" and "plays the game of politics." When I see this data, I mostly think to myself, who cares? The electorate had high hopes for Kevin Rudd and Malcolm Turnbull, then ended up disappointed in both. When they voted for Tony Abbott as prime minister, I saw the voters choose a man they knew well and disliked because they just couldn't vote Labor after all the turmoil and leader-swapping. Tony Abbott was lauded as a highly effective Opposition leader but then went on to be a highly embarrassing prime minister. What counts is not whether people like Bill Shorten – want to have a beer with him or consider him to be a dynamic personality on TV – but whether he will lead this country with conviction and professionalism. Much of this will depend on the lessons he and his team have learnt from the disasters of the Rudd/Gillard years.

When we think of these years, we are understandably preoccupied with leadership struggles, group dysfunction and failures to communicate well with the public. Failures of policy and philosophy are often secondary. And yet it is clear that in 2007 the newly minted Labor government had a chance to renew the social-democratic tradition to suit modern Australia. At the beginning of Kevin Rudd's first stint as prime minister, academics Jennifer Curtin and Craig Simes argued that "if social democracy is not in crisis in Australia it is at least in heavy disguise."

> The social democratic agenda of the ALP had been under severe stress since the demise of the Hawke/Keating Labor governments ... While in opposition the ALP did not challenge the continuation of free market policies or a partially deregulated labour market. They promised tax cuts and management of the economy in a way that would keep mortgage rates low, continued welfare to work programs, and dabbled with environmental and forest policies.

The mood for change at the end of the Howard era was overwhelming (recall the spike in the AES data in 2007 as an indication of political interest, hope and expectation) and the popularity of Rudd significant and broad-based. He could have been the leader to commence important, long-overdue work on the Labor Party's progressive vision beyond merely winning an election. He seemed the right person for the job: there was his affinity with Asia, his commitment to climate change and his personal interest in social issues such as homelessness. But he turned out to be a "good on paper guy." As Curtin and Simes point out, the ALP's 2007 election platform focused on inflation, interest rates and reducing government spending. And redistributive goals were to be achieved through lowering tax thresholds, low interest rates and building a strong economy. From the start, Rudd sold himself as a fiscal conservative and acted as a fiscal conservative – John Howard-lite. This was understandable, given that Labor desperately needed an election win and wanted to convey to the voters that the transition from Howard's Coalition after so many years wouldn't be a risky one.

The global financial crisis gave Rudd not only a focus – much like an election campaign – but also a chance to strut his stuff globally while arguing domestically for strong government action to avert disaster in the form of a complex stimulus package. Ironically, the package worked so well that the electorate didn't give Rudd and his team enough credit for it. While the unemployment rate remained below 6 per cent and the economy kept bubbling along, the electorate assumed it was the mining boom, the strength of the banks, and luck (unlikely to be repeated) that helped us avoid a recession. Once the crisis receded, Rudd's troubles really started. He and his team struggled to sell the merits of various aspects of the stimulus package (tough, I concede, given News Corp's relentless campaign against the Building the Education Revolution program). They struggled to sell the mining Resource Rent Tax (despite public support for such a measure). And then, of course, Rudd struggled to keep his own team and his own resolve when it came to the emissions trading scheme. His now-famous retreat from a carbon price is something he will have to wear forever, but the Labor leadership more broadly must shoulder some of the blame. If media reports are to be believed, it only took a few focus groups in western Sydney to turn Labor decision-makers around on a position that was central to their landslide win a couple of years before. Perhaps this showed that despite the interest in the environment shown by federal Labor in the 1980s and early 1990s, commitment to conservation and climate change had not penetrated Labor's social-democratic DNA deeply enough.

The economist Richard Denniss doubts that Rudd was a committed social democrat. "His commitment to climate change made him look like a progressive, but he never was." For Denniss, one of the most obvious signs that Labor under Rudd hadn't changed its economic framework since the 1980s was that when the cash was handed out in the first wave of stimulus to counteract the global financial crisis, one group of Australians missed out: the unemployed.

Viewed through a social-democratic lens, the policy achievements of the Gillard government were an improvement on her predecessor's. With roots in the industrial left in Victoria, she was willing and able to pursue the National Disability Insurance Scheme and the carbon price. But she also cut welfare payments to single mothers. Whether or not Rudd or Gillard were genuine social democrats was, in the end, probably irrelevant. Neither of them could provide stability to a party intent on tearing itself apart. Leadership turmoil, the loss of government and the reversals and undermining of critical policies mean the social-democratic legacy of the Rudd/Gillard/Rudd governments is weaker than it could have been. To me, this shows how important reform of internal structures is to parties in government. Because toxic factionalism had not been adequately addressed, it affected the ability of the Labor government to pursue its policy agenda.

Enter, stage right, Bill Shorten after the inevitable loss in 2013 – a faction man, a conventional political player. Labor under his leadership has made unprecedented commitments to revenue-raising and, when compared to previous Labor Oppositions, has advanced reform ideas that are quite bold. The commitments made at Labor's conference are almost a shopping list of the issues Australians want addressed. It shows that the key decision-makers either know how to read the research or have a good gut feel about what matters to the electorate. Or a bit of both. They are "not for turning" from their negative gearing policy, despite consistent pressure from business and the media and changing conditions in the property market. They have already committed to establishing a federal anti-corruption watchdog: a National Integrity Commission. If Shorten were to endorse tentative moves by some inside Labor to impose a cap on donations from corporates and unions, it would be ... surprising. Few political players who benefit from the current system want to change the rules. That will take concerted public pressure and perhaps a few more scandals, with parliamentarians resigning in disgrace or being carted away to prison.

After the celebrated Labor win in the seat of Longman (which saw a 13 per cent swing against the Coalition candidate and a 7 per cent swing towards Labor) the veteran journalist Barrie Cassidy remarked that Bill Shorten's strength is that people constantly underestimate him. And perhaps an unlikely hero is exactly what Australia needs after almost a decade of political turmoil and dashed hopes. Perhaps his unassuming style also fits a country with such a practical, undoctrinaire approach to democracy. Perhaps what Australians want is a steady hand, a leader of a team, an unremarkable but professional person who grows into the job, in for the long haul but seemingly unfussed at the start about the big legacy. Who knows? It worked for John Howard.

*

On the Australia Day weekend, as I caught a plane from Sydney to Melbourne, I came across an article in the inflight magazine by Tim Winton, his love letter to Australia. "What I love most about Australians ... [is] their capacity to learn and change," he wrote.

> We are all travelling, learning, growing. Whether we're conscious
> of it or not, we're on our way from something to something else.
> And along the way, we tend to ditch bad ideas and pick up better

ones. Most often these changes are incremental, barely felt. Sometimes they're traumatic. But the thing I remind myself of is that we
do move on. We change. We're actually pretty good at it.

I spent a long time reflecting on whether I agreed with these sentiments. I am still not sure. We have not changed enough when it comes to
addressing the legacy of colonisation and its impact on Australia's
Indigenous people. We've failed to reform the laws that govern our elections and political parties, even as public perception of corruption has
increased. The ethnic make-up of our society has changed a lot in the past
twenty years; the ethnic make-up of our parliaments has not. But I do
know that our tendency to resist certain changes can sometimes be a good
thing. We still hold onto fairness as a defining national value. We still support compulsory voting, even though we are increasingly cynical about
the outcome of that voting. The practical approach to democracy remains.
We still believe that government can play a productive role in people's
lives, delivering services and improving the chances of the collective to
thrive (sometimes even at the expense of individual rights). Much that
was described by W.K. Hancock all those years ago remains, even with
less elbow room in our major cities. I also know that for many decades
now any shifts of opinion in our society, any of these incremental or traumatic changes, have been absorbed and taken up by citizens long before
they have been widely acknowledged by our political class or reflected in
our laws. Politics lags behind the democratic majority – on issues like
housing, the environment and electoral reform – causing increasing anger
at our parliamentary leaders for not, well, leading.

While the research supports my optimism about the opportunity to
renew social democracy in Australia, there are a few critical brakes on
progress. The first is that low- and middle-income earners will continue
to oppose increased taxation unless governments fully address inequalities
in the tax system – everything from imputation credits and negative gearing to large-scale corporate tax avoidance and white-collar crime. There is

high public support for more government intervention in the market and for certain policies that require large amounts of public money – Gonski, broadband, disability insurance, social housing and so on. And yet I suspect the phrase "high-taxing welfare state" would strike fear and resentment into the hearts of citizens already angry about corporate rorts and the high cost of living. The public will find it hard to believe that any political party that continues to take big money from corporate and wealthy individual donors is prepared to build a fair tax system.

The second brake is that public acceptance of the scale of the threat of climate change is not yet widespread. To address this threat will require mobilisation of all the community and government resources at our disposal. It will require personal sacrifice. The public is inching towards this realisation, but again, I believe many will push back against calls to dramatically reorient our society to meet the climate threat unless they are convinced that the most powerful are also prepared to mobilise their resources and make real sacrifices.

At the next federal election, we may see the gap between the views of the democratic majority and the agenda of those they elect to govern the country close more than just a little. But a renewal of our democracy will take more than just closing that gap. It will require the Labor Party to take a determined, almost fearless approach in arguing to the Australian people (especially younger Australians) that our democracy can deliver on its promise. And that will mean delivering on their own promises. Indeed, if Labor, and Bill Shorten as prime minister, follow through on the agenda laid out that week before Christmas 2018, then we will have something more than an "It's fine" government. And it will be about time.

ACKNOWLEDGMENTS AND SOURCES

Dedicated to Liz and John, for support, advice and an always open door.

Thanks to Hans van Leeuwen, Verity Firth, Leanne Smith, Richard Denniss, Ariadne Vromen, Ben Raue, Tim Beshara, David Marr, Sebastian Tesoriero, Linda Scott and Rose Jackson; to the research agencies that have supported me over the past few years, including Essential Media and now CIRCA Research; and the talented researchers I've worked with, in particular Chris Strods, Kate Whelan, Tiina Raikko and Josh Rebolledo; and to the clients who commissioned the work and approved the inclusion of that work in this essay. A special shout-out to my husband. I made the unique decision to write much of the first draft of this essay on a twelve-day cruise to New Zealand, during which our four-year-old twins refused either to swim or go to Kids Club and our ten-year-old came down with gastro. He juggled it all on the high seas while I worked the laptop in the cabin. And finally to the great team at Black Inc. and the wise and patient Chris Feik.

2   "reconcile capitalism": Matthias Platzeck, Peer Steinbrück and Frank-Walter Steinmeier, "Social democracy in the 21st century," Policy Network, p. 2.

4   "In fact, history shows": On the accuracy of the national polls at the last federal election, see Murray Goot, "National polls, marginal seats and campaign effects," *Double Disillusion: The 2016 Australian Federal Election*, edited by Anika Gauja, Peter Chen, Jennifer Curtin and Juliet Pietsch, ANU Press, Acton, 2018. Goot is critical of seat-based robo-polling in his article, as are Simon Jackman and Luke Mansillo in an article in the same collection. They state that "seat-specific polls are subject to substantial biases, so much so that the typical seat-specific poll should be treated as if it had just one-sixth the nominal, stated sample size of the poll." This is not to say there aren't issues with social- and market-research methodologies that can produce erroneous results, but merely to note that the inability of pollsters to predict the last American presidential election or the Brexit result doesn't automatically mean there are the same problems with Australia-based polling.

5   "no consistent evidence": Of course, the nature of marginal-seat campaigning means that often a party might focus on the issues of swing voters in those seats

rather than on what these national polls and research reports are saying. So, instead of looking at all the aggregated polling data and ensuring policy is guided by that, the party looks at what research is telling them about a small but critical group of voters. But even that small group of voters is getting wise to this tactic: consider the backlash to the decision to move Australia's embassy in Israel to Jerusalem taken during the Wentworth by-election in 2018 and seen as a cynical move to appease a section of voters in a formerly Liberal enclave.

7   "actually *decreased*": Australian Electoral Commission, *Informal voting: 2016 House of Representatives elections*, www.aec.gov.au/Voting/Informal_Voting/.

7   "so slight": Samuel Hannan-Morrow and Michael Roden, "Gender, age and generational effects on turnout in Australian federal elections," Australian Political Studies Association 2014 Conference, Sydney.

7-8 "A majority of voters": Sarah M. Cameron and Ian McAllister, *Trends in Australian Political Opinion: Results from the Australian Election Study 1987–2016*, School of Politics & International Relations, ANU College of Arts & Social Sciences, 2016.

8   "80 per cent": Support for compulsory voting in Australian gradually increased during the 1940s, 1950s and 1960s, and has remained relatively stable since then. See Cameron and McAllister.

8   "the most distinctive characteristic": John Hirst, *Sense and Nonsense in Australian History*, Black Inc. Agenda, Melbourne, 2005, p. 310.

8-9 "Almost nine in ten Australians": Jill Shepherd, Ian McAllister and Tony Makkai, Australian Values Study 2018.

9   "Research commissioned by the Museum of Australian Democracy": See Gerry Stoker, Mark Evans and Max Halupka, "Trust and democracy in Australia: Democratic decline and renewal," December 2018, www.democracy2025.gov.au/documents/Democracy2025-report1.pdf.

12–14 "Social democrats acknowledged", etc: John Keane, "Money, capitalism and the slow death of social democracy," 17 May 2016, www.johnkeane.net/money-capitalism-and-the-slow-death-of-social-democracy/.

13   "A recent report": Australian Council of Social Services, "Inequality in Australia: A nation divided," 2015, www.acoss.org.au/inequality/. The data crunched for this report came from the well-respected Household, Income and Labour Dynamics in Australia (HILDA) survey. There is an energetic debate about whether economic inequality is rising and by how much. Wealth and income inequality are different beasts and the ABS has come to slightly different conclusions to HILDA and other surveys. Nevertheless, ABS data (a larger dataset than HILDA) shows inequality has risen. See Peter Whiteford, "Here's why it's so hard to say whether inequality is going up or down," *The Conversation*, 2 August 2017.

15 "what is living and what is dead": Tony Judt, "What is living and what is dead in social democracy," ABC Radio National, 2 May 2010.

16 "ensure that all people": Centre for Policy Development, "What do Australians want?: Active and effective government fit for the ages," December 2017, https://cpd.org.au/wp-content/uploads/2017/12/Discussion-Paper-Final-December.pdf.

18 "Australian democracy has come": W.K. Hancock, "The Australian democracy," in *The Words That Made Australia: How a Nation Came to Know Itself*, edited by Robert Manne and Chris Feik, Black Inc., Melbourne, 2014, p. 45.

18 "because there was nowhere else to look", etc: Hancock, p. 43.

19 "the desire for equality": Hirst, p. 149

19 "Free markets", etc: Keane, 2016.

22 "quite strong opposition": The Essential Report also suggests a divided electorate, with 39 per cent supporting income tax cuts and 30 per cent wanting the reversal of cuts to school and hospital funding. However, support for reversing these cuts jumps to 46 per cent among people with incomes under $600 a week.

28 "In 2018, the Essential Report": On restricting negative gearing and rental costs, there were similar findings: 14 per cent thought it would lower rents, 37 per cent increase them (naturally investors would pass on the loss of their tax benefits to their tenants), 24 per cent thought it would make no difference and 26 per cent said they didn't know.

28 "research project I did in early 2018": The project was for the Australian Institute of Superannuation Trustees, and included a survey of the general population and interviews with negative gearers and their kids. See www.aist.asn.au/policy-research-archive/research-papers/2018-research/home-truths-negative-gearing-and-retirement.aspx.

33 "one of the most useful": CSIRO, "Annual surveys of Australian attitudes to climate change," www.csiro.au/en/Research/LWF/Areas/Social-economic/Climate-change/Climate-attitudes-survey.

35 "More than 50 per cent": Aaron Patrick, "More than half of Liberal MPs don't trust climate science, think tank," *The Australian Financial Review*, 17 July 2017.

35 "care about the natural world": The CSIRO research found that "people's opinions about climate change are related to voting behaviour, but more strongly related to their environmental worldview."

36 "a fundamental challenge": Keane, 2016.

39 "living in a frightening new world": Richard Flanagan, "Tasmania is burning: The climate disaster future has arrived while those in power laugh at us," *The Guardian*, 5 February 2019.

42 "immigrants improve": Scanlon Foundation, 2018 *Social Cohesion Report*, https://scanlonfoundation.org.au/current-research/.

46 "Australia will struggle": George Megalogenis, "Rookie PMs," *Australian Foreign Affairs* 5, February 2019, pp. 74–5.

46 "Instituting the Uluru proposal": The Voice would be a representative body to advise parliament on policies affecting Aboriginal and Torres Strait Islander people, a central recommendation of the Uluru Statement from the Heart.

46 "By addressing the righteous demands": Indeed, part of improving our democracy has to involve breaking down current barriers to electoral participation by Aboriginal and Torres Strait Islander voters, which remain substantial. They include, according to the AEC, literacy and numeracy levels, cultural activities, school retention rates, health and social conditions, transience and remoteness. Restrictions on the right of prisoners to vote exclude a disproportionate number of Aboriginal and Torres Strait Islander people from voting. And how engaged can we expect Indigenous Australians to be in a political and parliamentary system given the legacy of bad decisions and inaction? Hopefully the fulfilment of the Uluru Statement will also involve a renewed push to understand and improve electoral enrolment and participation.

47 "one in four Australian ministers": Christopher Knaus, "One in four Australian ministers go on to work for lobbyists or special interests study finds," *The Guardian*, 24 September 2018.

48 "three in five Australians"; Inga Ting, "Ipsos Survey: Australians want a strong leader to take country back from rich, powerful," *The Sydney Morning Herald*, 17 January 2017.

48–9 "Money in politics", etc: Carmela Chivers, Danielle Wood and Kate Griffiths, "Time for the federal government to catch up on political donations reform," *The Conversation*, 14 August 2014.

49 "the gambling, alcohol and tobacco industries": Esther Han, "Gaming, alcohol, tobacco firms pour millions into political parties," *The Sydney Morning Herald*, 27 November 2018. See also Howard Pender, "Corporate Political Expenditure in Australia," Australasian Centre for Corporate Responsibility, June 2016.

49 "Recent media reports": See Samantha Hutchinson and Kylar Loussikian, "Labor eyes electoral reforms to stamp out big donors," *The Sydney Morning Herald*, 20 January 2019.

51 "Since the 1990s": Judith Bessant, Kerry Carrington, Mark Chou, Brendan Churchill, Anna Copeland, Anita Harris, Lesley Pruitt, Nathan Manning, George Patton, Steven Threadgold, John Tobin, Ariadne Vromen, Rob Watts, Anj Wierenga, Dan Woodman and Johanna Wyn, Submission to the Joint Standing

Committee on Electoral Matters on the Commonwealth Electoral Amendment (Lowering Voting Age and Increasing Voter Participation) Bill 2018.

54   "if social democracy is not in crisis", etc: Jennifer Curtin and Craig Simes, "Social Democracy in Australia," country fact sheet in the context of the project *Adjusting the Profile of Social Democracy in Europe*, 2008 at http://library.fes.de/pdf-files/id/ipa/05636-20080910.pdf.

57–8   "what I love most": Tim Winton, "What I love about Australia," *Qantas Magazine*, January 2019, p. 57.

Bri Lee

I suspect I am not alone in feeling confronted by Sebastian Smee's essay. If I'm honest, I bought it hoping it might give me a bit of a spook. For a while now, I have felt uneasy about the growing effect social media has on my work and life. I am twenty-seven and although I finished high school one or two years before smartphones became commonplace, I am still a "digital native," part of a generation for whom the internet is not a *place* you *go*, but an inextricable thread through the fabric of life itself.

Since my own book (a memoir about sexism in the Australian justice system) was published in June 2018, my Instagram account has become the key portal through which I communicate with my audience. Hundreds of direct messages have been sent to me from (mostly) women who have survived, or supported a survivor of, sexual violence. The platform is important to me and I am grateful to be able to hear from readers, but my Instagram account ballooning in reach has changed the way I go about my life. In a good way, I find myself looking for beauty, as I did when I was first learning about photography many years ago. In a bad way, if I am not careful, it changes how I visit art galleries and how I feel about my body. It makes me think I need to be one "type" of writer for my bio, or one "type" of woman for a consistent aesthetic throughout my feed, or even to live a certain "type" of always-on-the-go life that is constantly "engaging."

As Smee wrote, "the software knows how to make us want it." Without conscious monitoring, my use of social media expands and my priorities gradually shift, like icebergs, towards what is "shareable." I wonder if I can write hard-hitting legal analysis alongside fashion week coverage, or if people who follow me won't appreciate the "randomness" of my work. I buy more clothing. I walk a different way to the bus. I think about the cover of a potential book before thinking about what I actually want to write. Without deliberate rejection of this current, I do indeed feel myself "flattened, constricted and quantified." I don't like it.

But what kind of writer would I be without the internet? I think probably a broke and lonely one. And who am I to bite the feed that feeds me?

I do not make any assumptions about what Smee has or has not experienced in his life, but in his mentions of #MeToo I feel he understates the power of the internet to allow previously disempowered, disconnected people to find each other and share their stories. Articulately, he acknowledges that "attending to our true selves may reveal things we don't want or can't bear to see," and this is especially true for survivors of trauma. There is no "before" and "after" in making peace with complex internal elements of trauma or identity. It is a gradual fumbling towards the light, often made easier by connections that might be impossible to forge in real life. Online spaces can be liminal worlds for those simultaneously reaching outwards and inwards for understanding. Smee writes about the internet leading us to "betray" the inner self by our own "eagerness to make ourselves smaller" and "somehow less real," but for many people the internet allows them, finally, to define themselves. Online spaces can lend courage and understanding to people who then carry that deeper self-respect out into the street.

None of this has touched upon the legal issues surrounding software surveillance and information gathering and misuse, which could easily be the subject of a separate Quarterly Essay. Jaron Lanier's new book, *Ten Reasons to Delete Your Social Media Accounts Right Now*, cites plenty of alarming evidence of the genuinely evil goals of the companies that run these platforms (and he would know, because he was on the ground working in Silicon Valley at the dawn of what we now consider the internet). Interestingly, I found Smee's words more perturbing than Lanier's. I have always known that I am selling my data to Facebook, but it is only recently that I have begun to wonder if I am also selling it my heart and soul.

Finally, I want to return to a word and idea Smee chose that I am particularly interested in: the "betrayal" of the primary, inward experience. This sits at the core of my feeling of being confronted by the essay: the idea that the preciousness of the inner life can be spoiled by the big bad world if we do not fight to protect it from tainting. I feel this, but I have also written and published a terrifyingly honest memoir; in doing so, I flung my darkest personal truths into the starkly lit public square that is the internet. What is the difference? Is a part of our disdain for social media just a hangover from British/colonial sensibilities: the sense that "private things" should remain private? No, not totally. My book was born of commitment to myself. My Instagram remains a perpetual commitment to audience. So writing is my art and social media my commerce, and I am one of a million who feel panicked when their art is compromised by commerce.

Art has always struggled through eras of technological advancement, and it is up to us as artists to accept the challenge. Not to ignore the new stuff, but to grow through and rise above it somehow. If we consider the internet the enemy, then we have already lost.

Bri Lee

Briohny Doyle

Sebastian Smee doesn't feel like an algorithm. He feels more like a character in one of Chekhov's short stories, or a quality of attention in a painting by Cézanne, or even, at moments of digital overload, like the electric hum that passes between the unhinged and sinister occupants of Ryan Trecartin and Lizzie Fitch's surreal post-internet art-films. As corporate entities vie for our attention and collapse human existence into data, Smee accesses his inner life via these works of art. Inner life is hard to pin down, though. It's to do with meaning, Smee asserts. It is imaginative, quiet and particular. It's not about production, though it can be creative. It's an undervalued part of our identities right now, as we scramble to broadcast our "selves" out into the white noise of culture. Critically, Smee demonstrates that inner life can be framed as a space of refuge and even resistance in late capitalism.

I'm sceptical of claims to authenticity – intimations of a real you behind the stage-lit scrim – but Smee's melancholy over neglected inner life suggests he thinks this realm is muscular, requiring discipline to strengthen rather than existing a priori in the manner of a Catholic soul. I can certainly get behind this and I suspect the higher-ups at Facebook and Twitter would too. They want us to work this muscle in a particular way. They are helping us to train. How long was Facebook in action before we started thinking in status updates? What impact does trimming our ideas and opinions to 140 characters have on their content and scope? Ruminating on art and literature seems like a sensible strategy to counter this training. But although developing our inner life seems unambiguously worthwhile, I don't hold with Smee's hope that it will protect us from corporate incursions into our privacy. Inner life is not hermetically sealed. It's a catchment into which the flows of everyday life swirl and bubble. This produces a particularly heady mix at present, but hasn't it always, at least to some extent?

If art communicates the richness of human experience, the diaries and note-books of artists show lives simultaneously riddled with anxiety and superficiality, even before the internet. On a Friday morning in June 1938, before sitting down to work on *The Grapes of Wrath*, John Steinbeck wrote in his journal, "I had wanted to hear some music but the washing machine is going and I'll have a fairly hard time. I would do it tonight but I must go to the dentist and my jaws will be battered. My whole nervous system is battered. Don't know why. I hope I am not heading for a nervous breakdown." The next day, he begins an entry with "My traffic fine was $2.50. Thought it might be twenty-five. But now to work."

Susan Sontag, who helped us read the dangerous metaphors of the twentieth century, had other things on her mind too. In 1960, she realised how bad her posture was: "It's not that my shoulders and back are round but that my head is thrust forward," and four years later, a list of her faults includes a special note: "NB: My ostentatious appetite – real need – to eat exotic and 'disgusting' foods."

Tennessee Williams, a playwright whose characters are often destroyed by a violent dissonance between their inner lives and the social structures they're embedded in, kept obsessive notebooks full of tweet-worthy confessions. "I have a periodically painful tooth that worries me," he wrote in 1936. "It is surprising that all of us don't go mad in this world."

For every hour Cézanne and Chekhov spent pondering nature and human interaction, and every hour we have been enriched in turn, there have been billions collectively whiled away in worry, distraction, ambition, pettiness, hypochondria, narcissism, lust over a maiden's ankles, or coveting the neighbour's goat. Is the internet making this worse? Certainly. The internet is sculpted in the image of present-day capitalism. Today, many of us have more time for leisure, but we feel more pressured to produce, consume and perfect. In the future, we may feel less pressured but will also likely have less time and energy, due to the realities of surviving in new climates, both political and environmental.

I was reminded, while reading Smee's essay, of the Spike Jonze film *Her*, in which lonely, perpetually networked characters in a not-so-distant future convene and even fall in love with artificial intelligences. For protagonist Theodore (who works appropriating the emotional lives of others by writing their love letters), the emergence of Sam, his AI "girlfriend," inspires him to relate to the world in profound new ways. In the end, though, the film reveals that human consciousness is too limited to access the infinite possibilities of existence, and Sam leaves to hang out with some more open-minded entities. Poor humans, we can only think one thought at a time, are limited in our communication by language, and are utterly unable to see beyond our selves. It is our tragedy and also our gift, as these limitations provide the conditions for art, and for love.

Writing about digital technologies tends to reproduce a ubiquitous contemporary conflict. We benefit from the internet, can see possibilities for further benefit, while also encountering negative effects. We are reluctant to unplug, even if this means disconnection from other, more meaningful aspects of life. Smee doesn't want to be a snob proclaiming high and low forms of experience, yet he can't help it and neither can we. We don't want to be nostalgic, but we ache for the imagined simplicity of lost worlds. We don't want to be alone, but we mourn the death of solitude. We grapple, we are conflicted, and then, sometimes mercifully, we are distracted.

Briohny Doyle

Raimond Gaita

Sebastian Smee has written a wonderfully rich and complex essay. It's hard to engage with it in a short response. That's not his fault. We are, he says, becoming estranged from concepts we need as we try to understand ourselves. In part, he thinks, along with Zadie Smith, that's because we have been shameless accomplices to the ways Facebook and other social media have undermined the conditions for their application. Those concepts defined what he fears is now "an exhausted and tattered humanism." They enabled us to explore, in ways that went deep, our inner life and who we are. Now, he believes, we have acquiesced in the diminishment of both in ways that serve the financial interests of social media and those who benefit from its unprincipled data-sharing. If he's right, then we don't know whether we are lost in a new conceptual landscape, looking back nostalgically at the one in which we grew up but to which we cannot return, or are still in the old one, also lost, because so much of it is in tatters.

Other forces play their part in eroding the conceptual ground from under us. Many people speak now of post- and trans-humanism. They tell us that the ethically inflected ways in which we speak of humanity ("Be a human being for once in your life," "Treat me like a human being," "He's a human being, not a monster," for example) are suspect and mislead us about what carries the ethical load. It's not humanity, they say, it's the concept of a person, or even more abstractly and therefore potentially more universally, the concept of a rational agent. We are reminded to speak of human beings *and other animals* rather than of human beings and animals. We are invited to welcome the future in which we join in full ethical companionship with robots. Instead of wondering nervously when robots will become like us, we should ask when we will become like them – when, for example, will we be able to replace damaged limbs and body tissue, including brain tissue, with whatever we make robots out of? Who does not hope for the day when a brain-damaged person will be able to recover fully with manufactured brain matter?

"Matter" is the operative concept rather than "flesh and blood," with all the resonances that has had for us ("You're my own flesh and blood" doesn't mean, though of course it doesn't deny, that you're a biological relative of the same animal species). Smee refers to a friend who said to him, "We are all just basically algorithms." It's hard to know what that means other than being a gesture towards the kind of materialism that looks upon our embodiment as inessential to whatever ethical and other attributes we need to treat some robots as our friends, fully our moral equals. Smee says he is also materialist, which doesn't seem to come to much more than denying that we possess immaterial souls or minds, but he is ambivalent towards what his friend said. He says it bores him, even when he thinks only a little about it (a short paragraph in the essay), and with deflationary irony he reports that he doesn't *feel* like an algorithm. Nonetheless, anxiety about and resistance to the reductionist implication of his friend's remark keep resurfacing in the essay. He asks, "Is the resistance I feel [to thinking of himself as an algorithm] an old, sentimental and deluded way of seeing things . . . That old idea of 'nature,' those paintings." But when you read his wonderful description of the faces of the teacher and her pupil in Chardin's painting, it's hard to believe he is uncertain about how important it is that we are beings with faces to look into. "Does a bird have a face?" a philosopher used to ask students who were being interviewed for places in a philosophy department. It was a good question. The human body, Wittgenstein said, is the best picture of the human soul. He wasn't referring to an immaterial substance, no more than we are when we speak of soul-destroying work.

Who belongs to the "we" to which he and I refer? It doesn't express an empirical generalisation: it's an invitation. Smee makes that explicit: "Every day I spend hours on my phone. We are all doing it, aren't we?"

He cites no empirical studies, though there are plenty, many of them depressing. I don't think that's a failing. Nothing important that he says is vulnerable to empirical refutation, not because he is thoroughly on top of the empirical studies, but because his is a reflection in a different cognitive realm. The task he has set himself is conceptual, though not as it was for philosophers in the heyday of conceptual analysis (and now for that matter). For philosophers (for the most part) and empirical psychologists (for the most part), art is extrinsic to the cognitive character of what they do. They sometimes find it helpful, providing examples (usually ethical) to the former and hypotheses to the latter. But when one reads Smee's discussions of Chekhov, Roth, Bellow, DeLillo, Munro, Chardin and Cézanne, all of them a joy, it becomes evident that they (the artists and the kind of discussion he offers of them) are essential to the kind of understanding he seeks. Smee writes beautifully. He writes English "at full stretch," to take an expression from the philosopher Cora Diamond. In that kind of writing, style and content are inseparable. It's writing that can be seductive, and can move us to consent to things we realise later, after reflection, that we shouldn't have consented to, perhaps because our ear for tone or for what rings false is undeveloped, or perhaps because we were sentimental, as he fears he may be when he reflects on how he thought of nature. The need to overcome such failings defines and disciplines a distinctive sensibility. To render oneself answerable to it is to be engaged in one kind of "trying to see things as they are."

That's not how Ryan Trecartin and Lissie Fitch see things. I agree with Smee that they are brilliant filmmakers, but I could not find my feet with them (another metaphor from the humanism that tells us we have to find solid ground if we are to have any hope of being critically sober). In the comment thread of *I-Be Area*, someone wrote, "This is the best thing I've never understood." I found that interesting: the person who wrote it might let the work flow slowly and subconsciously in his mind, allowing it to resurface now and then. Eventually – it could take years – he might say, "Now I understand," which, of course, might not be true. That's how it is with much of our thinking about life. Sometimes, when we do not understand everything that others say at the time they say it, we trust what they say enough to allow it to enter our lives, to find, in its own time, ways to engage with what we already know and with our capacities – emotional, intellectual and spiritual – for understanding. A number of times in his essay, Smee reminds us that we often learn most deeply when we are moved by what people say or do, in life or in art.

When I was a student, a teacher, Martin Winkler, said something to me that shook me, to the core it turned out. I was defending a friend who expressed a prissy, condescending conception of social responsibility, disdainful of what he called the "mass hysteria" of kids at a Beatles concerts in the 1960s. Winkler detested what I was defending. He listened for a long time. Just past midnight, he placed his hands on the table, leant forward, holding me fast in a look I could not avoid, and said, "Gaita. Do you know what the core of responsibility is? It is responsiveness to the needs of another in a lived encounter." (I'm quoting from memory.) I didn't understand what he meant, but was profoundly moved. He said I should read Martin Buber's *I and Thou*. I didn't understand that either. Almost thirty years later I dedicated my first book to Winkler. I could have subtitled it, "Responsiveness to need." I'm still grateful for his loving severity.

Winkler probably knew I didn't understand, but he trusted that one day I might. To do that, he had to trust that I wasn't seduced by his charismatic personality, powerfully expressed in his dramatic demeanour that evening. He cared for me and wanted me to learn to think for myself. He called me, as I have put it elsewhere, to "an individuating responsiveness," to be wholly alive and alert, to answer and, later, to reflect critically on what he told me, allowing it to be informed by and to inform experiences that were my history and had made me who I was. That presupposes a collectedness in the present moment and over time that is not consistent with experimenting with multiple selves.

Smee quotes Mark Trade in the Trecartin and Fitch film that carries his name, saying, "The human era went like that, like a sweatshirt on a camp fire." Later Smee says, "Other truths emerge from these films like bats in the night." They speak, he says, to a sense that many people, especially teenagers, have that "no one is listening." Then he goes on to say that "the film proposes that no one need listen." If that were true, then Mark Trade would be right. Does that sound like a new idea of humanity, one that transcends all ethically defining ways of speaking of our humanity, as post-humanists claim theirs does? Or does it sound like old-fashioned dehumanisation?

In a fine essay called "Human Personality," Simone Weil asks, "What is sacred in every human being?" She rejects a number of suggestions and says:

> At the bottom of the heart of every human being, from earliest infancy until the tomb, there is something that goes on indomitably expecting, in the teeth of all experience of crimes committed, suffered and witnessed, that good and not evil will be done to him. It is this above all that is sacred in every human being ... Every time there arises from the depths of a human heart the childish cry, "Why am I being hurt?" then there is certainly injustice. Many people do not hear it. For it is a silent cry that sounds only in the secret heart.

Later in the same essay, she says of those who "have suffered too many blows" that "the place in the heart from which the infliction of evil evokes a cry of surprise may seem dead. But it is never quite dead; it is simply unable to cry out anymore. It has sunk into a state of dumb and ceaseless lamentation." That is hard-headed, truthful description of how it is for many asylum seekers and others who suffer severe and degrading affliction because we have found no need, or decided not, to listen.

Smee quotes Galen Strawson summarising Iris Murdoch's argument in her *Metaphysics as a Guide to Morals*:

> We are limited, imperfect, unfinished and full of blankness and jumble ... We are divided creatures, distracted creatures, extended, layered, pulled apart, our minds are like ragbags ... We cannot see things as they are.

Maybe we human beings are mostly a mess. After Freud, we can hardly think that is not true to a considerable degree. But Murdoch did not believe that we have lost the concepts that enable us to see the mess *as* a mess and to aspire to something better, even if often we don't have the desire to. Though she believed we are incorrigibly resistant to seeing things as they are, she did not think that there is no such thing as seeing things as they are rather than as they appear from the many false perspectives into which we are seduced or bullied by the "fat relentless ego." But, of course, what it is to see things as they are will be different for different domains of inquiry and reflection. In physics, it is one kind of thing. In literature, it is another. To see the reality of another person, she says, is a work of love, justice and pity. Obviously, reality is an ethically loaded term for her. So it is for Smee when he speaks of moments when reality becomes "really real" for us.

Often we ask ourselves, "Who am I really?" Or, "What would people think if they knew me as I really am, if they knew some things I think, feel and desire?" Or, "Do I really love this person, or is my passion one of love's many counterfeits?" On such occasions, we know more or less how to go on thinking further about these questions, how to sharpen them and how to look for answers, perhaps alone or in conversation with someone close to us. But whether we are doing it well or badly, we don't come to a point where we think we have to ask "What is the self?" in order to go further. If we do, we will not get further. The questions we ask on such occasions, what we do to try to understand what we are asking and what would count as an answer – all that gives sense to our talk of "the self," "selfhood," the "true self," and so on. To put the point in a way that engages more explicitly with Smee's essay: it is the elaborations of the forms of our inner life and the questions they pose that give sense to talk of "the self," rather than the other way about. There is no object that is the self; no thing with properties whose discovery could provide answers to any deep questions about ourselves and our relationships to others.

We are elusive to ourselves for different kinds of reasons. There are almost infinitely many ways we lovingly give ourselves up as victims to the fat relentless ego. At other times, it is because we do not fully understand the concepts that inform our most important beliefs and commitments, because they go deep in our tradition, whose influence on us is far from transparent. How many people, for example, realise the role that Kant has played in their belief that people possess inalienable dignity, or the role the Socratic idea that it's better to suffer evil than to do it plays in their suspicion that morality and politics are at critical times irreconcilably in conflict? Then, the question "Who am I?" has a different point, prompted by intimations that our beliefs may be informed by concepts richer or poorer than we presently know. When it turns out to be richer, we are grateful. When we realise that it's poorer, we may come to see that concepts to which we appeal can no longer have, or have only a muffled, speaking voice in our life with language. I often hear discussions of academic freedom that presuppose a concept of the university that has been defunct for many years. On this, as Smee says of concepts he fears we have lost, there appears to be no going back.

But there is also something different and deeper at issue in his discussion of the elusiveness of the self, although "elusive" is probably not the word with which to try to capture it. It is the wonder – I'd say mystery if I didn't fear to be misunderstood – of what it is to be a human being. Pablo Casals wrote in his autobiography that every morning for eighty years he went to the piano and played two preludes and fugues of Bach. He said it was "a sort of benediction on the house" – "a rediscovery of the world of which I have the joy of being a part." It filled him "with a feeling of the incredible marvel of being a human being … I do not think that a day has passed in my life in which I have failed to look with fresh amazement at the miracle of nature."

Few things I know are written more wonderfully in the key of gratitude. Casals' love of the world strikes me as the expression of a humanism that Smee would like to celebrate (and actually does). I don't believe our culture is dead to it. Certainly young people in their late teens whom I teach are not, though they are all on their smartphones when I walk into the lecture theatre. Nourished by Bach (though not only by him), Casals speaks of "the miracle of nature" as Smee would like to speak of nature enriched for him by his love of paintings. He is more anxious than he needs to be. He has written his humanism into a language he has helped to flourish rather than struggle to remain alive.

Despite the talk of post- and trans-humanism, people speak more often now than even ten years ago, I think, of humanity in ethically inflected ways. Certainly one hears people speak more often of our need to recognise the full humanity of all the peoples of the earth. Even the expression "Be a human being for once in your life," spoken as a rebuke or a plea, suggests that our humanity is something we are called upon to rise to, that it is not something given once and for all, as species membership is, nor can some of us finish the task of becoming human by the time we are, say, fifty. The call to rise to our humanity would not cease if we lived a thousand years.

There is more than one form of love of the world that is important to Smee's essay. To illustrate what it is, I'll finish by quoting Hannah Arendt. She also helps me to place the significance of the extraordinary last lines of Smee's essay. He quotes Chekov:

> "All that I now write," he continued, "displeases and bores me, but what sits in my head interests, excites and moves me." Chekov was talking, of course, of his inner life. And in these simple, unforced statements, he showed how dearly he wanted to protect it.

Now Arendt. The quote is from "On Humanity in Dark Times," published in her book *Men in Dark Times*:

> [The] world is not humane just because it is made by human beings, and it does not become so just because the human voice sounds in it, but only when it has become the object of human discourse. However much we are affected by things of the world, however deeply they may stir and stimulate us, they become human for us only when we can discuss them with our fellows. Whatever cannot become the object of discourse – the truly sublime, the truly horrible or the uncanny – may find a human voice through which to sound into the world, but it is not exactly human. We humanise what is going on in the world in ourselves only by speaking of it, and in the course of speaking of it we learn to be human.

Raimond Gaita

Fiona Wright

To say upfront what needs to be said: I am a millennial. I am a millennial, and this response will probably seem solipsistic, and it will be fragmentary. It's not that I can't help it. It's not my attention span, my inherent narcissism. I'm just making a point.

*

I went to a party on New Year's Eve, a fairly small party, at my friend Theo's house. Early on, I started chatting to some people hanging about in the kitchen, near the chips, near the cheese; I asked them how they know Theo and one said, oh, I know him from Twitter. Yeah, me too, said another.

I know Theo as a friend-of-a-friend, and I found out later that the friend who introduced us also met him on Twitter. And he was new to Sydney, he adds, so we went out for a drink.

In the hour before midnight we all dance in the front room, loose-limbed and sweaty and silly, and we laugh, hard, at the playlist we've all added tracks to. The air feels close and warm and like a heartbeat.

*

On Facebook, I have a group of men and women whom I met in hospital, as well as men and women I haven't met who've been admitted there since. We ask each other for advice, for recommendations of dietitians and psychologists, we share frustrations and small triumphs and those niggling awful thoughts that only people who know this illness understand. It's these people I go to when I can't stop thinking that I should stop taking my meds because I've decided they're making me hungry. It's these people I go to when I fit back into my older, larger swimsuit, and feel triumphant and terribly sad, both at once. And yes, we share photos of food – but here they mean something powerful, something exultant, something extraordinary.

*

On Instagram, my artist friend is cutting up old canvases to stitch them into something new. Another is hanging her show in Dubbo and her beautifully detailed miniatures look like the scales of a giant sea-creature, silvery and somehow fluid, there on the wall. My friend, a burlesque dancer, posts photos from the class she teaches, a line of women, all shapes and sizes, laughing and shimmying. A photographer, some glossy stills from a recent shoot, low-lit landscapes, eerie and plangent. None of these I would ever, otherwise, have seen.

*

On Facebook, I have a group of writers who share job opportunities, and competitions, and calls for pitches and submissions, who share book and research recommendations, warnings about dodgy clients, advice about pay rates, commiserations over rejections. One writer is working on a PhD proposal, so I send her mine to use as a model. Another isn't sure if the word he's using is a regionalism, and within an hour has responses from all across the country, confirming or denying that it's used there. I need access to a university library, and someone loans me their credentials. We're freelancers. We have no job security, no company resources, no employers. But we do have each other, and this feels important.

*

On Instagram, I follow an account where women – it doesn't explicitly say they're women, but they so obviously are – post screenshots of the awful or disgusting or just generally creepy messages that men on Tinder send them (the sender's name always obscured), and this feels revolutionary.

On Instagram, I follow an account where a woman, an ordinary-looking, unmade-up woman, takes photos of herself beaming and holding junk food – a Heineken beer she calls "green juice," three broken-open crème eggs labelled as a "protein breakfast," a Bounty chocolate bar captioned "coconut and cacao bite" and this feels revolutionary.

*

Through Facebook, a woman in the States has organised both the funds to pay a migrant woman's bail and a convoy of volunteer drivers to take her across the breadth of that country to where her children had been taken after they were separated at the border by migration officials. So many people offered money, offered help, that she has since arranged to do this for many more women, to provide them with legal aid, assistance with housing, amenities, clothes.

On Twitter, I read about a woman raising money to pay the fines of impoverished Indigenous women mandatorily imprisoned in Western Australia for being unable to make those payments themselves. Five thousand people donate in four days. Thirty women are set free in the same time. This isn't clicktivism. This is defiance.

*

On Instagram, a poet friend takes photos of her semi-industrial suburb – concrete driveways, wire fences, bougainvillea gone rampantly wild – and is using them to write a new collection. On Instagram, a novelist friend takes photos of details of suburban houses – art nouveau friezes, dichromatic brickwork, porticos and pebbledash letterboxes – and uses these to write his debut. On Instagram, a writer friend takes photos of old-fashioned and outmoded Sydney buildings – a dusty milk bar on Parramatta Road, a mushroom-shaped reservoir towering above Petersham, a roller-skating rink, a civic centre – and maps these in her work. These books are smart and literary, thoughtful and odd, and full of joy and longing.

*

On Twitter, last year, I started following people writing about chronic illness and disability, and I read and I read: their posts, their links, their articles. On Facebook, I joined a group of writers with chronic illness and disability, and I read, and I learned. I would not have been able to come to terms with my own illness, to think of and accept it as disability, without this, not at all; and this is a revelation.

And all of this is inner life.

Fiona Wright

Correspondence

Ashleigh Wilson

Last April, when Mark Zuckerberg visited Washington to testify before the US Congress, he looked penitent but prepared. Zuckerberg had come to take responsibility for Facebook and explain how the personal data of its users would be better protected. He performed well enough, though there wasn't a lot he could say to stop public opinion turning against him. It was turning against his peers, too. The world's technology giants have been looking anything but benign recently, which is why the executives who run them have gone on the defensive as never before.

At the same time, a collective recalibration has been underway about the devices attached so intimately to our lives. Like poker machines adorned with hotlines for problem gambling, these products now come with health warnings.

If digital devices are harmful – psychologically, physically – the consequences may not be clear for years. This seems especially the case when we consider the interior spaces that Sebastian Smee explores in his elegant, disturbing essay. Who knows: by the time these maladies have been diagnosed, it might be too late.

But as I read his essay, following a trajectory that roamed from Instagram and Twitter to Francis Bacon and Chekhov – pausing every ten pages or so to check my phone, occasionally scrolling past social media posts from Sebastian himself – I found myself thinking about a related issue: the gradual disappearance of downtime. For the first time in human history, we have the capacity to fill every waking moment of our lives. Is it possible, though, that we're giving up something along the way? Perhaps there's a cost to creativity when we no longer allow our minds to float.

Those health warnings give us reason to pause. In 2018, Apple released an updated operating system that included Screen Time, a feature that tracks how long we spent on our devices. (It also has an option to "schedule time away from the screen.") Is Screen Time meant to make us feel empowered? For me, those notifications prompt a very different emotion: shame. It's difficult to justify a daily average of 2 hours 53 minutes, as my recent update tells me, even if I tell myself that repeated visits to Instagram, Twitter, Gmail and Chess.com are essential to my day. But I suspect there's another reason for the shame. It's a niggling feeling, a distant sense that something is slipping away. Perhaps it has to do with losing touch of the messy details that make our worlds so colourful and unknowable, the "gritty precipitate," as Sebastian puts it, of our lives.

Last year, Google announced its own suggestions for "digital wellbeing." This was one of its tips: "Schedule custom breathers as often as you want, pausing what you're currently watching and encouraging you to step away."

The problem, though, goes deeper. It's one thing to circumscribe your social media use during work hours or stop answering emails from bed, but it's something else entirely to allow ourselves those brief spaces between all this activity when once we would drift, lost in our thoughts.

Look around: passengers on a bus, lost in their phones; office workers colliding on the street; customers in a lunch queue, head down, scrolling.

I don't mean to be judgmental: I do this too. But not so long ago, we filled these gaps in our lives – commuting, waiting for a lunch, long drives, walking – with our thoughts. Now the gaps are closing, and I fear we're losing our ability to sit and think. To let our minds wander. To daydream.

This is not an argument for meditation, where the goal is a state of mindlessness, or an internal stillness. I'm referring to those meandering jumbles of thought that can lead, every now and then, to clarity, and even to art.

Many years ago, I used to complain during long drives through the Queensland bush, and my late grandmother always responded the same way. "Only boring people get bored," she said, and I rolled my eyes every time.

(By the way, I should come clean about my Screen Time update. My recent average was 3 hours 20 minutes, half an hour more than the number I quoted earlier. Yes, I downplayed my average.)

There's a passage in *Shell*, the 2018 novel by Kristina Olsson, in which a Swedish glass artist is on a ferry heading towards the Sydney Opera House, still under construction. He's baffled by the indifference of the other passengers: "To him, even now, the Opera House rose up like an idea as the ferry approached the quay, something he'd dreamed and was slowly remembering. He didn't want to lose that sense of the place, wanted never to feel it as so familiar that he would sit on a ferry and look away."

Nick Cave, the songwriter, reflected recently about the way great trauma can rob an artist of his or her "sense of wonder." He was answering questions from fans on his website, and on another page he responded to a question about creativity. "Ideas are everywhere and forever available," he wrote, "provided you are prepared to accept them."

This brings to mind a lecture I attended two decades ago at Sydney University. I wish I could recall the lecturer's name, but he was talking about Emily Dickinson, specifically her hummingbird poem:

A Route of Evanescence,
With a revolving Wheel –
A Resonance of Emerald
A Rush of Cochineal –
And every Blossom on the Bush
Adjusts its tumbled Head –
The Mail from Tunis – probably,
An easy Morning's Ride –

I remember him luxuriating in the wonder of these words, encouraging us to see the poet dreaming about the whirl of colour and movement. Dickinson was writing a long time before the Wright brothers began their experiments in the sky, and this, I think, was my lecturer's point. He was telling us about the power of imagination. Before we can create an object, we need to imagine it. And how better to imagine flight than by reflecting on the majesty of the hummingbird and then to wonder what it would take to harness such power, to travel on the wind, to send messages from the most exotic parts of the globe in the time it takes for an easy morning ride.

Ashleigh Wilson

Correspondence

Melanie Joosten

Until I read *Net Loss*, I had not considered the possibility that my inner life was damaged beyond repair. I was holding onto the belief that not clicking on ads made me unfathomable to advertisers, that turning off the notifications on my social media apps rendered me immune to the internet's deleterious effects. I thought I was safely standing at the edge of the vast ocean of the internet's subsuming mediocrity, just dipping my toes in, admiring the view. Reading Smee's essay, I realised I was already drenched in online distractions. I was possibly even drowning (definitely not waving), and it was time to get serious about nurturing my inner life lest it disappear altogether.

Cannily, Smee puts readers like me at ease with his confession that he spends hours on his phone every day. This was kind reassurance that he would not be preaching from some higher place beyond the wifi signal. In an eloquent but never patronising manner, he argues that all this mindless scrolling is insidious, damaging our minds and filling them with detritus, so that we can no longer judge what is important and what is not. We are in danger of spending so much time preening our surfaces — our Instagram-ready light-drenched homes, our aerial shots of nourishing foods, our long-haired children with their wooden toys and organic cotton rompers — for the viewing pleasure of others that there is no room within our minds for what makes us feel truly seen or understood, what snaps and sparks our intellects into the service of joy.

Net Loss touches on the way being a parent or being in a marriage can bump rudely against one's inner life; how even as these relationships provide a sense of ballast and happiness they are essentially in competition with the self. Reading this, it struck me that the heavy weight of mothering (yes, mothering, not just parenting — don't @ me), brings an even more consuming threat to a robust inner life than just the perilous distractions of social media — a double whammy, if you will.

The quandary of looking after young children is well known: so much time spent on tasks that require little more than your presence and, consequently, so much time to think about all the intellectually satisfying things you could be doing if you weren't pulling errant textas out of the subwoofer, coaxing a nipple into a teething mouth or cleaning smooshed banana from the couch. Claudia Dey describes it perfectly in an essay in *The Paris Review*:

> The private actions of the mother's mind – her scholarship, perversions, miscellany, narcissism – are swamped by the bureaucracy of parenting. A ticker tape hurtles across the mother's brain listing all of the things she must remember: spoon, bathing suit, milk, booster shot, sign-up, pickup, 3:15. These lists are a form of paying attention, which is a form of love. Love, a wise woman once told me, is how you make the other person feel. Love is how you make your child feel. You accomplish the list. And then the list, indomitable, grows anew.

She speaks the truth. I have just spent twelve months on maternity leave with my second child and among the antics, the terror of the growing list and a lack of adult conversation, I often found myself reaching for my phone, desperate for a signal from the outside. Or even better, a "like" of one of my social media posts, carefully constructed to prove that I was still a functioning part of the world "out there," which now seemed so distant.

Increasingly I realised that these distracted dips into the online world were making me feel listless – sometimes even useless, jealous, pathetic or sad – rather than invigorated. My hyper-awareness of all the voices in the online world was making my own world harder to be in. My daughters had laid claim to most of my time – I needed to ensure social media did not devour every remaining moment of the day, leaving me with nothing. So I stepped back. I stopped checking Twitter, I logged out of Facebook, and I looked up from the screen. Smee's essay came at just the right time to help me articulate why this was necessary.

I had believed everyone who told me that becoming a mother was going to be the end of my inner life. That changing priorities and the subsuming love would overpower any personal direction or desire. I knew I would no longer have time for the reading or writing that were integral to my sense of self; I was resigned to being reduced to the algorithm of first-time mother, even as I raged against it. Every time I opened my browser, there were ads for baby paraphernalia and links to articles about mothers: women who existed only in the service of their offspring. I couldn't see myself in them, but who else could I possibly be?

So I was genuinely surprised to find that when I had recovered from the bloody cleaving and splitting of my body, I was still very much the same person I had always been. I still wanted to read the same books, see the same theatre and start piecing together a new novel. It was the logistics that had changed rather than the desire – and need – for the activities themselves. I now write in small moments of snatched time or larger ones negotiated with my husband (also a writer). I try to avoid the time-suck of social media and make efforts not to search out reviews of every movie I've seen or book I've read, opinion pieces on what to be outraged by or where to direct my scorn. It's not easy; I'd become used to the piecemeal energy that the clamour of online distractions offered. Instead, I try to make enough room for my own voice, even if only within my own head, because otherwise I am shouting to be heard: at myself; at my children; at the void.

It is hard to put time aside to nurture my inner life, because it seems like an indulgence. By way of demonstration, Smee's essay refutes this, making the statement that consuming and creating art are important. His references to various artworks and how they make him feel and think attest to the worth of their creation and his taking the time to understand them. This is what I needed to hear. I write because it engages my mind, allows me to express things I must and gives me the opportunity to think on the page. Writing is an imperfect rendering of my inner life and indispensable to holding together my sense of self. The word "hobby" has always seemed too light, too diminutive for the pleasure and purpose that such activities bring, but I have begun to see that it is through my "hobbies" that my sense of self expands in a way that the reductive online world discourages.

Busier now, I cannot go to a gallery or read long texts without taking myself away from my children, even when in their presence. This is hard: not to resent the hours lost to playgrounds and swimming pools. So, in order not to isolate myself, I turn to my daughters to do some of the heavy lifting – I observe them being in the world and creating their own selves just as I might observe actors in a play, or an artist rendering emotions in paint. Smee's description of video artists Trecartin and Fitch is eerily and hilariously reminiscent of toddlers, who also demonstrate "what the human personality looks like when there is no inner life, when everything is externalised."

As the inner life of my three-year-old daughter forms, it bursts out of her constantly, her body and face expressing what she will one day learn to restrain. Watching her learn to "perform" her self, and to start hiding away some of her feelings, I realise that my inner life – this thing I cultivate in time away from my children – while so essential to my own being, will always remain obscure and unknowable to them. As it should. However, when Smee writes about the panic induced by the realisation of our aloneness, and that death will one day take with us whatever we regard as a soul or self, I wonder: am I guarding my inner life too fiercely? Recording an online version of oneself is a valiant attempt to share – to be seen and heard, to be a part of something. But it is damagingly reductive. Algorithms don't allow for the ambivalence, the nuance, the multiple truths. I want my daughters to grow up and accept the mess of life, not just cleaned-up data and identities shorn of subtlety and ambiguity.

So perhaps – in real life – I need to attempt to make the line between the inner and outer self more permeable. Sharing some parts of my inner life with those I am close to will give me less reason to seek the voices and validation of the online world. It may also strengthen and magnify my inner life – or at the very least, keep it visible to me.

Melanie Joosten

Imre Salusinszky

In *Net Loss*, Sebastian Smee worries that in the age of the internet the inner self is becoming "harshly illuminated and remorselessly externalised, and at the same time flattened, constricted and quantified." It is getting harder, he suggests, "to be alone with ourselves." He says one context in which the beleaguered inner life comes into play is "when we feel ourselves to be in an intensely charged relationship with things, or people, or works of art, that are outside us."

It seems to me that travel is a paradigmatic example of this context and illustrates what has been gained and lost in the era of the smartphone. I am talking here about what travel means, or meant, for young Australians last century. Remember what going overseas was like before the smartphone and the internet? Remember how cut-off we felt, travelling or studying or working overseas for a year or more? Remember hanging out for the weekly aerogramme from home, or the three-day-old VFL scores in the *International Herald Tribune*? When you went away in the 1970s, you really went away. The isolation was painful, but also bracing. We not only learnt a good deal about ourselves, but were also forced to engage with the cultures and places we were visiting, and of course with the strangers we met on the road.

Coincidentally, I read Smee's essay just as I sat down with my family for our annual viewing of the 1987 John Hughes comedy *Planes, Trains and Automobiles*. In this story of two ill-matched, accidental travelling companions, Neal Page (Steve Martin), a fastidious, upper-middle-class marketing professional, finds himself thrown together with a messy, unfailingly cheerful travelling salesman called Del Griffith (John Candy). Meeting as strangers at La Guardia airport, both men are headed to Chicago for the Thanksgiving holiday. A blizzard, along with other complications too numerous to summarise, sends them on a lengthy detour using the film's eponymous modes of transportation. At once a road movie and a buddy movie, with two genius comic actors at the top of their form, *Planes, Trains and*

Automobiles is ideal summer holiday fare. But almost nothing in the plot would work if you tried to re-make it today. Neal and Del would never end up spending their first stranded night sharing a double bed in a cheap motel in Wichita, because Neal would have used his smartphone to find somewhere classier to stay and promptly summoned an Uber to get him there (rather than the garish low-rider taxi provided by a friend of Del, who of course has been to Wichita many times). Using various travel apps, Neal would find ways to re-route his trip that didn't involve, among other improvisations, a ride in the refrigerated trailer of a meat truck. In short, the internet would provide Neal with whatever savvy and local knowledge was necessary to avoid entering into a reluctant partnership with somebody like Del.

Even if two such unlikely companions were forced to spend time together, in this century, Neal would find refuge from Del's incessant chatter in the online edition of *The New Yorker*, while Del could seek solace in the arms of YouTube. And, most crucially of all, Neal would be in constant communication with his wife and kids back home in Chicago – via emails, text messages, ironic selfies and voice calls – instead of being limited to issuing them rushed updates whenever he can find a payphone.

For Neal Page, a journey through the regional Midwest, sharing cheap motel rooms with an overweight battler, is also a journey to the limits of his patience and tolerance, especially towards those who do not share his social class and its attitudes. Del Griffith, meanwhile, comes to understand that overbearing bonhomie is not always the ideal approach for making a new friend. Through the experience of being alone, together, away from home, both men change, grow and learn.

Travel, before the internet, was rich with these experiences. It had something to do with our isolation from habitual personal and cultural supports, and the resulting necessity to find new ones. When we remain permanently "connected," most of this necessity disappears. We cannot be forced outside our comfort zone, because it is there in our smartphone.

The ubiquity of the smartphone, I suggest, marks the tipping point of the process Smee is worried about, in which our capacity for solitude, and whatever we may draw from it, has been disrupted. The internet, Google, email, even social media – none of these advances in information technology would have had their transformative effect if the smartphone had not come along and put them all in our pocket.

It's more than just the availability of the internet: our smartphones have us all "on call" 24/7. We are available. We can be summoned – out of reverie, out of solitude, even out of companionship. If you take an audit of a random crowd of workers leaving a suburban railway station in the early evening, as I sometimes do as I walk my dog, you will find that the vast majority of them have, in fact, been summoned out of solitude and reflection by their smartphones.

Of course I understand that it is still possible to travel, to explore, to learn and to change: not only possible, but, thanks to the smartphone and the internet, also cheaper and more convenient than ever before. But the character of travel has altered fundamentally, and as a result the inner self rarely finds itself confronted and challenged by personal and cultural isolation. *Planes, Trains and Automobiles* is barely thirty years old, but the world of travel it portrays is dead and gone.

In the age of Google Maps, our sons and daughters will never comprehend what Bonnie Tyler means when she warbles about being "lost in France in love." Whether this is actually a net loss is uncertain, given some of the positives, such as being able to carry the entire human archive with us wherever we go. But it is certainly a conversation worth having.

Imre Salusinszky

Sebastian Smee

I am not an optimist about the possibility of self-improvement, or even dramatic personal change, so I regret the extent to which my essay came over as a rebuke: *You are spending too much time online! You must change your life!*

What I really meant, of course, was: I am *spending too much time online. Help!*

Help is just the thing an online existence can offer, as Fiona Wright reminds us in her response, my favourite among all these generous and eloquent replies. I loved reading them all, but Wright's was my favourite. It felt like a just rebuke and it was wonderfully written: "In the hour before midnight we all dance in the front room, loose-limbed and sweaty and silly, and we laugh, hard, at the playlist we've all added tracks to. The air feels close and warm and like a heartbeat."

I found Bri Lee's description of online connections in the wake of trauma as "a gradual fumbling toward the light, often made easier by connections that might be impossible to forge in real life" utterly convincing. The passage in Briohny Doyle's response that included "We don't want to be alone, but we mourn the death of solitude" rang so true. I loved Ashleigh Wilson's description of the threatened status of daydreaming – "those meandering jumbles of thought that can lead, every now and then, to clarity, and even to art" – and Imre Salusinszky's evocations of the experience of travel before smartphones: "The isolation was painful, but also bracing."

Somewhere in my essay I acknowledged the upside of social media, but I consigned it to a single paragraph. Lee is right: I "understated the power of the internet to allow previously disempowered, disconnected people to find each other and share their stories." So let me state clearly that I don't think social media is inherently bad. Not at all. It's the drive to profit from it and the ensuing business model that, to me, looks bad – even disastrous. Part of the reason I wrote *Net Loss* was simply to join a growing chorus of voices sounding the alarm about these business models. I wanted to urge people to go beyond the naivety that treats social media companies as innocent platforms and insists, "But it's central to my life and so helpful" – all of which is doubtless true – and to acknowledge instead that this experience, both individualised and collective, is part of an unfolding, society-wide crisis. I do not, as Lee suggests, "consider the internet the enemy." That would be tilting at windmills. I use the internet every day, I depend on it, and I want, what's more, almost all the things that Wright, Lee and Doyle value. I value them too.

I am worried, rather, about the companies that harness internet technology in order to profit from it, and the effect this is having on all of us. There is no doubt that these companies provide a compelling user experience. But that experience is also, in many cases, dangerously addictive – and not by accident. It is made to be so. This is affecting our children, who are more or less defenceless against the power of the gadgets we give them. In fact, I believe it is changing the very nature of childhood.

It is also affecting society at large, on a scale we are struggling, I think, to understand – in part because we don't want to understand. Facebook is the punching bag du jour, but that's because Facebook, which also owns Instagram, had 2.32 billion monthly active users last year. That's almost a third of the world's population. Instagram, meanwhile, has more than 1 billion active monthly users. (And yes, I got these figures from the internet.)

Facebook's 2.32 billion users place their trust in the company. Its profitability depends on that trust, which Facebook converts into "surveillance, the sharing of user data, and behavioral modification," in the words of Roger McNamee, an early Facebook investor and the man who introduced Mark Zuckerberg to Sheryl Sandberg. Facebook exploits vulnerabilities in human psychology to manipulate attention, because that's how it makes money. If it did all this as a neutral platform, which it claims to be, that would present a difficult problem. It would be difficult because Facebook has frequently made itself "neutrally" available to bad actors who weaponise it, amplify prejudice, undermine democracy and incite violence, sometimes – as in Myanmar – on a horrific scale. But the premise is wrong, because Facebook is not even close to being neutral. Facebook starts out, according to McNamee in his book *Zucked*, "giving users 'what they want,' but the algorithms are trained to nudge user attention in directions that Facebook wants. The algorithms choose posts calculated to press emotional buttons because scaring users or pissing them off increases time on site. When users pay attention, Facebook calls it *engagement*, but the goal is behavior modification that maximizes engagement and therefore makes advertising more valuable."

Facebook is the fourth most valuable company in America. It has detailed profiles on every one of its users. It is controlled by a young man who, during the company's period of maximum growth, did not believe in data privacy, who sought only to maximise user growth, engagement time, disclosure and sharing because he knew that his company's value derived from these things.

The implications are massive. Remember: 2.32 billion active monthly users. "Behavioural modification" on this scale might make us all happier, healthier, more connected. Or it might not. It might instead lead, for instance, to changes in government. The results of the Brexit referendum and the US election triggered analyses showing that Facebook, in McNamee's words, "conferred advantages to campaign messages based on fear or anger over those based on neutral or positive emotions."

America is living with the results right now, in the form of a raging, infantile president, a corrupt and inept cabinet, a judicial system that looks set to change American society for decades to come, and a widespread, atavistic assault on science, journalism and truth itself.

This worries me. And since every social media company – not to mention every government with authoritarian leanings on both the left and the right – is learning from Facebook's business success, I worry that down the track, we will only have to worry more.

But did I write my essay because I care so deeply about social media, its uses and abuses?

Not really. Each to his or her own. My wife is active on Facebook and uses it to keep her relationships with family and friends back in Australia meaningfully alive, whereas I, who have deleted my Facebook account (and never used it for personal purposes anyway), struggle to keep up with friends back home. Dear friends. Why? What's my problem?

I wrote the essay more, I think, to find ways to talk about an obscure feeling I have, and have always had, of being somehow inside myself – full of thoughts and feelings, some exuberant, some melancholy; some simple, some absurdly elaborate – yet being unable, except in rare moments of consolation or bliss, to connect those feelings with other people.

Unable or (and here's the strange thing) unwilling. Because often the feeling I have is that I don't want to share, that what is in my head is too special, too precious to share – and that by inference, perhaps, I am too special and precious. This is a kind of narcissism, to be sure.

But it is also what I meant by inner life. We are all, I think – and to a larger extent than we like to admit – islands. No one is carrying around the same experiences in their heads that I do. No one has anything like the same experiences and feelings as my mother, or my father, who are now in their seventies. When they die, we will talk about how special and irreplaceable they are, how much has been lost. But why not talk about it now? They are both utterly unique – not just their genetic make-up but the things they have experienced, learned and read, the things they have made with their hands, the places they have been, the languages they speak, the patterns of connection inside their brains, the things that have most moved them, their inner lives.

"Only connect!" exhorted E.M. Forster (one of the great describers of inner life). But aren't missed connections so interesting!

When I was in my early twenties and feeling low, a concerned family member suggested that I do some volunteer work, just to get me out of my own head. It was good advice. I took it. My aunt had a contact at the Children's Hospital. I went along and for a few days worked on the adolescent ward, where the kids who had eating disorders and were long-term patients were gearing up for a party. My job was to help out – garland the place with paper ribbons and so on – but also (ironically, given my own state of mind) to try to contribute a bit of festive cheer. I knew nothing about eating disorders and didn't learn much either. But I got to know one of the girls there. She was unwell, bedridden, very thin, but making progress. She had been hospitalised for several months.

The part I remember most vividly is when she had a visitor, who was also a teenage girl. The visitor had been to a Madonna concert the night before, and was coming in to tell her friend about it. She had auburn hair, light freckles and a slight accent I couldn't place. Until a few days earlier, she had been a long-term patient herself. Through the trial of hospitalisation, the two girls had clearly formed a close, mutually supportive friendship. The visitor had made good progress and been released. Her friend still had a way to go. Their conversation that day was awkward, sweet, hopeful, sincere. They didn't seem to mind me being there, although perhaps they were just being polite.

The tough part came when it was time for the visitor to leave. Both girls put a brave spin on it, but the farewell was full of sadness, in mutual acknowledgment of a cleaving reality: you are free to go, I have to stay; you got to dance the night away at the Madonna concert, I get a pathetic party in this hospital ward; we formed a life-saving bond; you are now leaving me with this random guy, these nurses, these doctors.

The point of my telling this story? I suppose I am trying to signal that I think I understand Wright's explanation of the benefits of Facebook, and that I understand that yes, all of this online activity is also inner life – urgently so. Had it existed all those years ago, social media would likely have helped the visitor and her friend, providing practical help for survival, ameliorating their separate struggles by fusing them, as much as possible, into a shared struggle – the very definition not just of community, but of something like love.

But I am also still thinking about the problem of connection and the strange dynamics of being there and not being there. This dynamic, which haunts our online existences, but also our lives more generally, somehow remains at the heart of what I was trying to say.

There is a woman in an Alice Munro story who finds herself at the checkout in a small town's general store. She presents her unusually big pile of groceries to the woman at the cash register, who says – with a "comradely sort of envy" – "You must've brought home company."

"When I wasn't expecting it," confirms the woman, adding (of men): "What a lot of bother they are. Not to mention expense. Look at that bacon. And cream."

"I could stand a bit of it," says the shopkeeper.

It's odd, I know, but the shopkeeper reminds me in some strange way of the girl on the ward listening to her friend's account of the previous night's Madonna concert. "I could stand a bit of it," she seemed to be thinking that day, in her comradely sort of way.

And I felt a similar thing myself while reading Wright's description of dancing in her living room. One of the most beautiful things I have ever seen was a man and a woman dancing at a party. I would write about it (they were dancing together, sweaty and loose-limbed, for more than an hour, their movements and the thing that was going on between them so intimate and extravagant at the same time, and I, a terrible dancer, like a shameful voyeur, couldn't look away because it was like looking into a fire: I felt I was looking at life itself) but if I say more I will surely betray that feeling, and anyway, this is not the occasion.

Sebastian Smee

Briohny Doyle is the author of *The Island Will Sink* and *Adult Fantasy*. She is a lecturer in writing and literature at Deakin University.

Raimond Gaita is a professorial fellow at the University of Melbourne and emeritus professor of moral philosophy at King's College London. His books include *Romulus, My Father, Good and Evil: An Absolute Conception, A Common Humanity, The Philosopher's Dog* and *After Romulus*.

Rebecca Huntley is one of Australia's leading social researchers. From 2006 until 2015, she was the director of the Mind & Mood Report, Australia's longest-running social trends report. She is now head of Vox Populi research. Her most recent book is *Still Lucky*. She presents *The History Listen* on ABC Radio National.

Melanie Joosten is the author of the novels *Berlin Syndrome* and *Gravity Well*, and the essay collection *A Long Time Coming: Essays on Old Age*. She works in social policy with a focus on older people, elder abuse and family violence.

Bri Lee is the author of *Eggshell Skull*. Her writing has been published in *The Saturday Paper*, *Crikey* and *The Guardian*.

Imre Salusinszky was media director for the former NSW premier Mike Baird. His biography of Rev. Dr Evan Pederick, who came forward and confessed to his role in the 1978 Hilton Hotel bombing, will be published later this year.

Sebastian Smee is the author of *The Art of Rivalry* and art critic for *The Washington Post*. He won the Pulitzer Prize for Criticism in 2011 and was a runner-up in 2008. His writing has appeared in *The Boston Globe*, *The Australian*, *The Sydney Morning Herald*, *The Monthly*, *The Guardian*, *The Independent*, *The Times*, *The Financial Times* and *The Spectator*.

Ashleigh Wilson has been *The Australian*'s arts editor since 2011. His first book was *Brett Whiteley: Art, Life and the Other Thing*. His next is *On Artists*.

Fiona Wright is a writer, editor and critic. She is the author of two collections of essays, *Small Acts of Disappearance* and *The World Was Whole*, and a poetry collection, *Knuckled*. Her poems and essays have been published in *The Australian, Meanjin, Island, Overland, The Lifted Brow, Seizure* and *HEAT*.

www.ingramcontent.com/pod-product-compliance
Lightning Source LLC
Chambersburg PA
CBHW050442300326

41934CB00044B/3412